MAGAZINE

MAGAZINE
The biography

MAGAZINE

MAGAZINE

Written by Helen Chase
Designed by Malcolm Garrett

Malcolm Garrett

379/1000

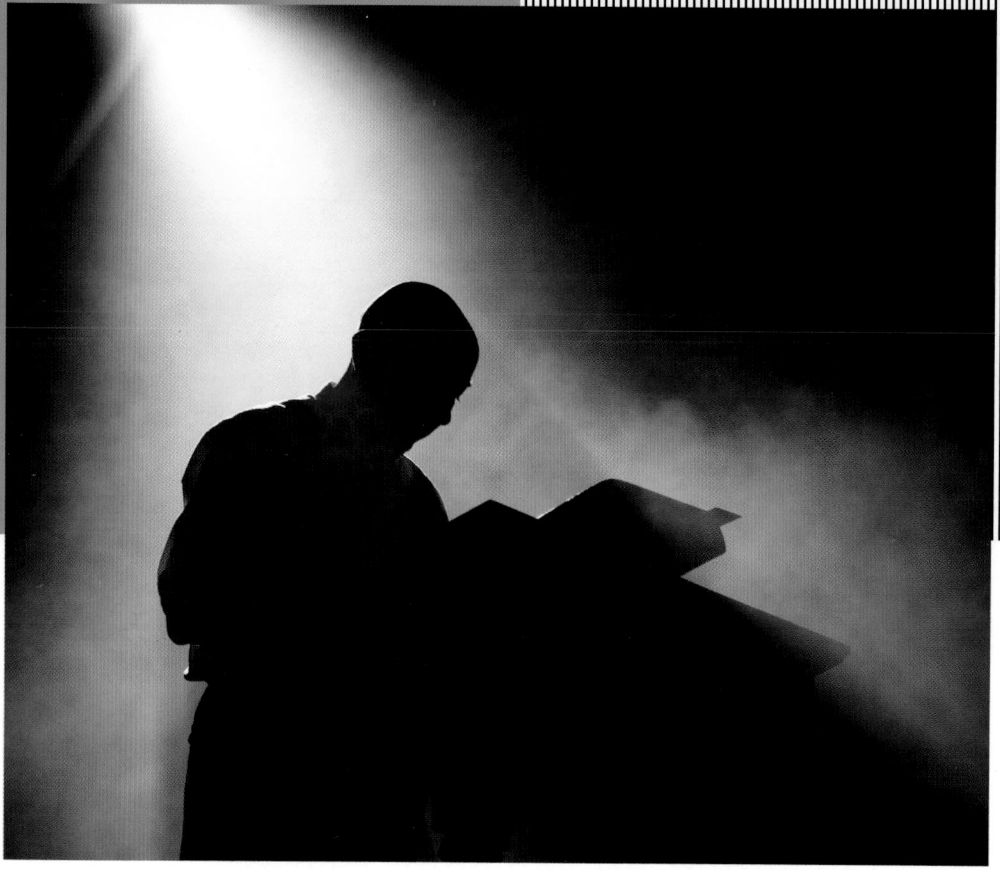

northumbria|press

Published by Northumbria Press
Trinity Building, Newcastle upon Tyne NE1 8ST

First Published 2009
© Helen Chase
Designed by Malcolm Garrett RDI ©2009
Typeset in Venus and Garamond

A catalogue record for this work is available
from the British Library.

ISBN: 978-1-904794-43-1

Printed by Graphicom srl
Viale dell'Industria 67, 36100 Vicenza, Italy

Contents

CHAPTER ONE	– Introduction	2
CHAPTER TWO	– The Band	20
CHAPTER THREE	– Shot By Both Sides	40
CHAPTER FOUR	– Real Life	62
CHAPTER FIVE	– Secondhand Daylight	88
CHAPTER SIX	– The Correct Use Of Soap	102
CHAPTER SEVEN	– Magic, Murder And The Weather	118
CHAPTER EIGHT	– After The Fact	126
CHAPTER NINE	– Reunion	140
CHAPTER TEN	– Artwork & Sleeve Design	156
APPENDIX ONE	– Lyrics	169
APPENDIX TWO	– Chronology	197
APPENDIX THREE	– Discography	205
	– Acknowledgements & credits	216

—

The biography

Chapter One —

_____

Here is
the lie
of the land …

Introduction

MAGAZINE WAS FORMED by Howard Devoto in 1977 and brought together some of the finest and most innovative musicians of the era in the core line-up of Devoto, John McGeoch, Barry Adamson, Dave Formula and John Doyle. Original and ground-breaking, Magazine had its roots in punk but had a greater emphasis on lyrical content whilst combining elements of avant-garde pop, funk and rock. Although achieving critical success in their four years together, commercial success largely eluded them. However, Magazine were and are a greatly respected and hugely influential band and their music remains fresh and relevant today.

Magazine came together in Manchester and played their early gigs in the local venues which were still throbbing with the aftermath of punk. Manchester has often been referred to as a 'music' city and the modern history of the place is inextricably tied up with the development of music in the area. Local musician, writer and lecturer CP Lee says, "It is uniquely placed in the history of popular music because it repeatedly jumps in feet first into great music, great scenes and on an international level. If you look very closely you can see the tracer bullets being fired throughout history."

CP Lee points to the influence of Jewish culture, Celtic elements and folk elements on the city's musical identity and in common with other historians he argues that music was an important part of the working-class culture. He describes how in the 1950s the proximity of Burtonwood American Base led to an influx of American jazz musicians feeding into existing groups in the city and how by the end of the decade the influence of American recording artists like Muddy Waters led to the development of beat music and beat groups. By the early 1960s there were over two hundred live venues in the Manchester area. Although the city was overshadowed for a time by Liverpool with the success of The Beatles, venues like The Twisted Wheel and The Band On The Wall gained reputations as some of the best places to play and hear live blues music.

The opening of Strawberry Studios in Stockport put the north-west spotlight firmly back on Manchester as it developed into one of the busiest and most successful studios in the country. Peter Tattersall first acquired the studio in 1967 and it operated as Inter-City until 1968 when further investment by Eric Stewart (then of The Mindbenders, later of 10cc) brought about a revamp and a name change. Much of 10cc's success was due to the fact that they were able to take their time recording, and experiment away from the pressures and financial constraints of the London music business.

Although the studio was successful and acted as a magnet to bring bands to the Manchester area, the live scene had dwindled. An Act of Parliament – the 1965 Corporation Act passed on January 1 1966 – had put paid to many of the live venues as the city fathers feared a subversive influence at work on the city's youth. In 1972, in an attempt to redress this situation, Victor Brox organised a meeting at the Bierkellar, which led to the founding of Music Force – a socialist organisation and musicians' co-operative. The stated aim of Music Force was to help musicians take control of their destinies by providing transport, renting out PAs and helping out with advertising. CP Lee says, "There's always been a tremendous musicians' infrastructure here in Manchester that's enabled the different movements or genres or waves of music to happen and to continue and carry on so that one builds upon the other."

The image of late 1970s Manchester has to some extent been shaped by the mythology that has built up around bands like Joy Division. Photographer Kevin Cummins' celebrated images of the band were shot on a grey, bleak, snowy day in January 1979 on a bridge in Hulme. This image of Manchester was further romanticised by Anton Corbijn's biographical film of the band, *Control*. Certainly 1970s Manchester was a typical post-industrial city with large decaying warehouses and some ill-conceived city regeneration projects. But it shared these attributes with many other large cities.

Much has been made of the political climate at the time and its influence on the type of music that began to emerge from 1976. Campaigns like Rock Against Racism were set up as a response to an increase in racial conflict and the growth of white nationalist groups such as the National Front. Punk rock formed the soundtrack for the visual imagery of strikes, electricity shortages and rotting rubbish on the streets. Pronouncements from figures such as John Lydon that punk rock was a reaction to the oppressiveness of the system reinforced the relationship between music and political and social unrest. Whilst this might be true for some people, Howard Devoto's motivation for getting involved in music was personal rather than political – he once observed wryly, "In myself, I can't say that I was feeling particularly great at that time – but what's new?"

The early to mid 1970s is also often described as something of a cultural wasteland but although the music on the radio in the UK was dominated by glam rock bands and major groups like Led Zeppelin and Pink Floyd (who by this point seemed to represent the corporate face of rock) it was possible to look beyond that to the really vital music which led up to and pervaded this era. Speaking sometime later, Howard said, "There was some big elemental thing that happened with the Sex Pistols, but in terms of music there was a whole gamut of other stuff which I had liked, and which, in the realm of ideas, was not a totally different tin of biscuits – Leonard Cohen, Dylan, David Bowie." (*The Guardian*, 25 February 2000)

It is commonly acknowledged that it was the Sex Pistols' legendary gigs at the Lesser Free Trade Hall, which took place in June and July in 1976, that brought together many of the personalities who were to go on to shape the immediate future of music in Manchester and beyond. Despite the extensive documentation of these two gigs there remains uncertainty about exactly who attended each one. It is beyond dispute that founder Buzzcocks' members Howard Devoto and Pete Shelley were there – along with Steve Diggle – by virtue of the fact they promoted the gigs and played at the second. Amongst the thirty or forty people who showed up at the first were Morrissey, along with Peter Hook and Bernard Sumner (later of Joy Division and New Order) and Paul Morley who went on to write influential pieces about Manchester bands in the music press. Less clear is the attendance of Mark E Smith (The Fall) and Tony Wilson although they were present at least one of the gigs.

Broadcaster, journalist and music fan Tony Wilson has been credited with having a massive influence over the development of music in Manchester in the late 1970s. According to photographer Kevin Cummins, "He was like a kid when it came to music. He believed in bands when no one else did, and was prepared to spend his own money, making things happen. He was the catalyst for everything that happened on the Manchester music scene from the 1970s." (*The Observer* 12 August 2007) Certainly he was one of the few broadcasters prepared to give time to new leftfield music talent on his cultural round-up show *What's On* and the shambolic but iconic *So It Goes*.

Many fans who have stayed with Magazine to the present day were first introduced to the band through the programmes Tony Wilson presented. Although *What's On* was in reality a fairly mundane and parochial weekly round-up of local events, Tony Wilson transformed it into a slightly anarchic and whacky cult-show – with a snippet from Magazine's *Shot By Both Sides* as its introduction. It ran for several years with its peak in the late 1970s. Along with the parrots, camels and spider-man costumes that frequented the studio Tony would always manage to shoe-horn in a slot for one of his current favourite bands, probably much to the bewilderment of a large portion of the tea-time viewing audience.

Speaking to Andy Fyfe for *Q* magazine, shortly before his death in 2007, Tony said, "In 1976 Granada decided to do a *What's On* music spin off, hoping it would be a network ITV show to rival *Top of the Pops*. We did one pilot and they went, 'Well, it's not a *Top of the Pops* rival but we'll give you a late night series, and that was *So It Goes*." He continued, "Many things that people think were on *So It Goes* were actually on *What's On*. So for example when I wasn't allowed to have Blondie on *So It Goes* because the producer thought they were crap, I put her on *What's On* and she did *Rip Her To Shreds*."

The first series of *So It Goes* had a fairly unremarkable line-up, but the last programme in the series came after Tony had attended a Sex Pistols gig. He remembered, "I went back the next day and screamed to my producer that we had to have this band on the show, it was the most exciting thing I'd ever seen. They said okay, but I had to take Malcolm the researcher to see them to make sure he liked the band too. I remember bright blue skies driving from Golden Square in Soho to the Walthamstow Assembly Hall, and walking into the hall at 9 in the evening, still this bright sky, and into this completely dark hall, with 20 people watching in a semi-circle stretching across the whole hall. I soon realised that it was because John was gobbing and they were just out of gobbing distance."

Magazine featured in the Autumn 1977 series of *So It Goes* – along with The Jam, Elvis Costello and Iggy Pop. When Iggy behaved rather outrageously and Granada found itself in the position of fending off criticism from the network the programme was pulled in December of that year. Although Tony was to go on to bring other music programmes to the network – including *B'Dum B'Dum* the 1978 documentary about Pete Shelley and Howard Devoto and their respective bands – he was for a while bitter about the panning that *So It Goes* got from certain quarters. Speaking to *NME* in 1990 he said, "*So It Goes* was condemned by the entire daily, weekly and monthly press, with the exception of Chris Dunkley in the *Financial Times* and a second opinion in the *Daily Mail*. They hated me; they hated it; they hated everything! Once you've been that hurt, nothing can ever hurt you again."

Having rubbed shoulders with the musicians he was such a huge fan of however, Tony wanted to be part of the scene that was developing. His enthusiasm which, legend has it, far outweighed his business acumen, spawned Factory Records and later the infamous Hacienda nightclub. Together with Alan Erasmus he also founded Factory nights at The Russell Club – ostensibly a West Indian night club in the bowels of Hulme. For one night a week it gave a platform to the emerging punk and post-punk bands on the circuit.

By this time original punk rock venue the Electric Circus had been shut down by the authorities. Initially a heavy metal venue in the rundown area of Collyhurst to the east of the city, for ten months it had been hijacked by the punks who needed a venue for their new music. Strangers to the area approached the place with some trepidation as captured by this young fanzine writer: "Never been here before, frikin' hell what a dive. Area looks like Hiroshima a while back. Left the car two miles away (felt like staying with it). After queuing halfway back to Piccadilly... we got to the door. Only to find – that the joint was full. Somehow we managed to get in." With its closure however, venues like The Factory (Russell Club) were even more important in providing an outlet not just for bands from the north-west, but from other parts of the country too.

In these pre-internet days the importance and power of the music press was paramount. It has been calculated that in the mid 1970s the combined readership of music papers was two million. Speaking to musician and writer John Robb in 2006, John O'Neill of The Undertones says, "I cannot emphasise how important the *NME* was from 1974 to 1977. It was the highlight of my week. I was buying the *NME* and it was a lifeline. I was checking out who influenced who and where the music came from. It was impossible to hear these groups. I read about The Velvet Underground, and the only Velvet Underground record you could get in Derry was the one after Lou Reed had left." According to Simon Reynolds in *Rip It Up And Start Again,* "The writers intensified and accelerated the development of post-punk music. The stark urgency and clean lines of the prose mirrored the music and the record cover art." Local journalists and photographers like Paul Morley and Kevin Cummins ensured that the burgeoning Manchester music scene was well represented within its pages.

The DIY ethics that those early Sex Pistols gigs engendered also manifested themselves via the written word in the many fanzines that appeared on the streets. As John Robb comments in *Punk Rock: An Oral History,* "The photocopier was king, with primitive fanzines, posters and flyers benefiting from the new, fast and furious, cut up montages of high energy art and stencilled graphics that became a punk rock staple." One of the most famous fanzines was *Sniffin Glue* but Manchester fanzines such as *City Fun, Bombsite* (Manchester and Liverpool), *Printed Noises* and *Shy Talk* all added to the punk literacy of the time.

At the same time artists and graphic designers like Linder Sterling, Malcolm Garrett and Peter Saville were spilling out of Manchester Polytechnic and working hand-in-hand with the punk pioneers. Simon Reynolds writes, "The entire period looks like an attempt to replay virtually every major modernist theme and technique via the medium of pop music.." He observes, "The record cover artwork of the period matched the neo-modernist aspirations of the words and music ... with designers drawing from Constructivism, De Stijl, Bauhaus, John Heartfield and Die Neue Typographie."

Richard Boon and Tosh Ryan were also important figures on the Manchester scene. Richard Boon ran New Hormones, Buzzcocks' management company, whilst Tosh Ryan was a founder member of Music Force in 1972 and formed Rabid Records in 1977. But it was Geoff Travis at Rough Trade, in London, that formed one of the early conduits for the first punk singles. Once Buzzcocks and *Spiral Scratch* had set up the template for the punk DIY ethos, and paved the road for the decentralisation of the record business, Rough Trade played a vital role in facilitating the distribution of punk and post-punk records.

Pete Shelley, however, recognised the benefits of being removed from the

London based record business. Talking to John Robb he says, "I suppose it was good for us being in Manchester because we weren't tainted by the rush to sign once record companies thought they'd buy into this music and sign up anyone they could. London was more media orientated than Manchester. In many ways it was less competitive and there was less to fight over." He continues, "Because of Manchester's early involvement [in punk] it was a place where bands from London would want to play."

In 1976, Manchester was second only to London as a bastion of punk. But by 1977, punk had already become a parody of itself and Manchester was establishing itself as a centre for bands which would later be labelled together under the banner of new wave (at the time) or post-punk; along with Magazine, bands such as The Fall, Joy Division and others made a massive contribution to the late 1970s/early 1980s musical landscape – which in Simon Reynold's eyes rivals the fabled years of 1963 to 1967. He writes, "The post-punk era certainly rivals the 60s in terms of the sheer amount of great music created, the spirit of adventure and idealism that infused it, and the way that the music seemed inextricably connected to the political and social turbulence of the times."

On forming Magazine, Howard Devoto took with him the DIY and anti-establishment attitude of punk rock and the creative energy it unleashed, and harnessed it with a desire to do something more constructive and forward looking – and less self-limiting. Magazine fan and lead singer of 1990s group Mansun, Paul Draper, says, "Magazine were the first to mix that keyboard punk rock sound with intricate arrangements and emotional, intelligent lyrics with the angry punk ethic." For Johnny Marr, speaking on the Radio Two programme *Spellbound:* "Magazine stood out because they were slightly intellectual, they had the sound of their day, the currency of their day but they weren't thrashing around on bar chords or in leather jackets and to anybody in the know, there seemed to be a good idea going on there."

Although initially a product of the punk rock years, Magazine owed more to the bands that preceded the era, forming part of a lineage that runs from The Velvet Underground through Bowie, Roxy Music and what became known as 'Krautrock' – and runs forward to the crop of current bands who have embraced both guitars and synthesisers along with an art sensibility and intelligent lyrics. In June 1978, Chris Brazier wrote in *Melody Maker,* "With its astounding brightness and modernistic vitality, its transcendence of and isolation from current trends, its sheer compulsive brilliance, Magazine's first album takes up the stark white flame of Roxy Music, still arguably the best British group spawned by the 70s, and thrusts it firmly into an unsuspecting present."

Musician Norman Fisher-Jones (Noko) was a fan from the beginning. He says, "The most exciting times for me were those John Peel years, the post-

Bruce Gilden's Mardi Gras photograph (see page 124) was used on the first Magazine flyer (below) and then later on the cover of *Magic, Murder And The Weather* (page 210)

Flyer for first gig at Rafters in Manchester on 28 October 1977

New Manchester Review
at Rafters
The debut proper of

MAGAZINE
plus
The Fall
plus sideshows

Friday 28 October

Food, late bar and disco
Tickets from: Rafters, Oxford Street, and Virgin Records, Lever Street
Photo: Bruce Gilden

BARRY ADAMSON
bass guitar
HOWARD DEVOTO
vocals
MARTIN JACKSON
drums
BOB DICKINSON
keyboards
JOHN McGEOCH
guitar

Promotional flyer, 1977 *(autographed by the band)*

Harvey Goldsmith Entertainments
with the
New Manchester Review
present

MAGAZINE

PLUS SPECIAL GUEST
JOHN COOPER CLARKE
AND
THE NOSE BLEEDS

THE NEW RITZ
Whitworth Street, Manchester

Monday 8th May 1978

Tickets: Pandemonium, Black Sedan, Virgin, Hime & Addison, and Paperchase.

Left and below: press ad and promotional flyer, 1978

Right and following three pages: both sides of a large format promotional leaflet, 1977

Magazine

Some songs : Touch and Go · Motorcade · Burst · Shot by both Sides · My Tulpa · Shouting Legs · The Light Pours Out of Me · Suddenly We Are Eating...

Photos : Kevin Cummins
Lithograph : Odilon Redon

MAGAZINE TOUR

APRIL

24	GLASGOW	SATELLITE CITY
25	LIVERPOOL	ERIC'S
26	BIRMINGHAM	BARBARELLAS
27	BRISTOL	TIFFANYS
28	PLYMOUTH	METRO
30	CROYDON	GREYHOUND

MAY

5	SHEFFIELD	POLYTECHNIC
6	CARDIFF	UNIVERSITY
7	LONDON	ROUNDHOUSE
8	MANCHESTER	RITZ

Touch and Go/Goldfinger
A new single by MAGAZINE

Both sides of a promotional flyer for the Spring UK Tour, 1978

Sometimes it's worth living.

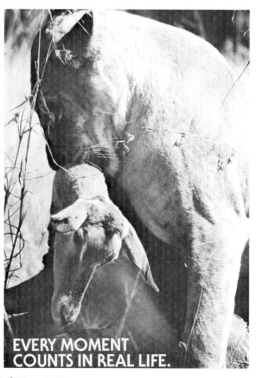

Each side of two promotional flyers for the Real Life Tour, 1978

punk years where you heard fifty things every night that were just completely vital from experimental, Cabaret Voltaire, Gang of Four, heavy dub – and Magazine were one of the groups that were locked in with all that. They were one of the first bands that actually did have the best of every one of those elements. They were as heavy as any band, they were as musically adept as any progressive band, they were as noisy as any punk band and they were as intelligent as the literature I was just getting in to." For Bob Dickinson, Magazine were "a catalyst for bands to cross over from one area to another in a very unselfconscious way".

Fusing the genres of punk, rock, funk and soul then, Magazine were, for many, one of the most experimental and innovative of the bands around in the late 1970s. Writing in *Sounds* in 1980 Dave McCullough said, "Along with PiL Magazine are one of the few bands championing and trailblazing the effective use of synths and moogs." Commenting after he had left Magazine, John McGeoch was also to say, "We were one of the first new wave bands to use synthesisers and when Numan emerged no-one gave us any credit for him ripping us off. We had an intense direction of no surrender which sadly didn't come across – it wasn't the kind of no surrender Sham 69 had – it just wasn't fashionable. I can only say these things now I've left."

The individual members of Magazine were and are excellent musicians in their own right. Guitarist John McGeoch has been mentioned as an inspiration by such contemporary artists as U2, and Red Hot Chili Peppers' John Frusciante has been quoted as saying that he taught himself to play "learning all John McGeoch's stuff in Magazine and Siouxsie and The Banshees". His guitar playing has been described as innovative, intelligent and distinctive with Siouxsie Sioux adding, "He had that great drama in his music that was cinematic."

In their time together between 1977 and 1981, Magazine were never to achieve mainstream success. John McGeoch reflected later in life, "Magazine were always a connoisseur's choice. We broke new ground, we set the tone for the next twenty, thirty years, but we never made much money". Impossible to pigeon-hole, the music press and wider public didn't 'get' them. They were however, very influential. John Leckie, who produced both Magazine and Simple Minds says, "Magazine was the inspiration for Simple Minds – along with other bands. In a way Simple Minds kind of mimicked what they were doing. There was a merging of the guitar and keyboard sounds. Charlie Burchill was looking to John McGeoch in the way he used his guitar."

Paul Draper of Mansun became aware of Howard Devoto and Magazine when he was a teenager and says, "I loved the use of guitar riffs and keyboards along with the rhythm grooves. It was a template for what I wanted to do musically." The members of Radiohead have long acknowledged the influence that Magazine had on their own musical development and sound. Writing recently on their official website, Jonny Greenwood said, "It's about time they got recognised for their song writing (which informs so much of what Radiohead do – no guitarist inspired me more than John McGeoch), and live performances (which we were too young to have seen)." John Leckie feels that he got the opportunity to work with Radiohead on their album *The Bends* because the band were so impressed with his work on Magazine's first album.

Influenced by his older sister, Colin Greenwood of Radiohead first got into Magazine via the third album *The Correct Use Of Soap*. He says, "I remember buying *Secondhand Daylight* from Banks Records in Norwich when I went to visit relatives and listening to it on my grandfather's record player in King's Lynn. I remember *Permafrost* and thinking this is quite heavy and kind of dark – but I preferred the more poppy, obvious stuff on *The Correct Use Of Soap*". According to Colin, the best thing the band ever recorded, because of its energy, was the live *Shot By Both Sides* recorded at The Russell Club. He says now, "That 12-inch was the most important record for us in our house".

As well as loving the soul influences in *The Correct Use Of Soap,* and the imagery, Colin was attracted by what he describes as "the combination of punk rock and opera – the histrionics, the ambition, the nihilism and romanticism." He was also fascinated by the dynamics of the key players in the band, "My impression of the band is that there are a lot of strong personalities because they're all such good players. He refers to "the sense of disaffection from Howard that came off every interview" and says, "I find those things interesting because I can draw comparisons with my experiences of being in Radiohead – seeing how a character can commit to working with musicians and perform in front of an audience but at the same time not wanting to engage with anyone in the media or press outside that forum that they've chosen to perform in."

As he grew up, Paul Smith of Maximo Park was aware of Buzzcocks but had yet to fully explore Magazine's music. It was in the early days of his own band that he was introduced to them as he relates, "Just before we got signed, a guy gave us £500 to get 300 copies of our first 7-inch printed up. He was an old punk and he was a big fan of the band. I remember him saying, 'You sound a bit like The Monochrome Set'. After watching us live a few times he said, 'You remind me a bit of Howard Devoto.'" This prompted Paul to actively seek out Magazine's music and he bought *The Correct Use Of Soap* – "probably because it was on offer in HMV".

He says, "The first song – *Because You're Frightened* – you're straight in there with a classic. I remember thinking this is a great band that has something extra. They're enigmatic – there's not much information, the band aren't on the front cover..." He continues, "When I listen to Magazine as I'm walking round the streets I'm aware of this kind of alienation from other people. We're all inherently apart from each other and what I like about Magazine's music is this acceptance of this apartness, this otherness and when I walk along the streets it chimes with what I see. I associate Magazine's music with built up areas. It doesn't depress me – it makes me feel stronger".

As well as admiring Barry Adamson's bass playing, Paul was seduced by the charisma and power of Howard Devoto's performance as a frontman (albeit only transmitted to him through the medium of YouTube) and it is something that he aspires to in his own role as frontman of Maximo Park. He says, "In Newcastle especially, from the beginning, what we were doing stood out from most people, because it was pop but it had an edge to it and an aggression. From the very first gig, when we played live I tried to get in the face of the audience rather than allow them to have a comfortable evening watching a band nodding along. That's the sort of thing I'd rather not waste my time on".

Paul Draper says, "Magazine are one of the most influential bands ever from the UK and always will be. Music goes in fashion circles and today's new wave influenced bands that came to prominence after Interpol broke big prove that Magazine's sound and influence will be regurgitated round and round forever. But the thing is – they were the first to do it and that is fixed in UK music history and the band's legacy will get bigger and bigger. Magazine's influence is all over today's music – just listen to White Lies, Editors etc etc, dark, brooding, intricate, emotional driven rock." John Leckie also recognises a revival of sorts of Magazine's 'sound' in the crop of current bands combining guitars and electronics.

It is clear that Magazine's music has stood the test of time – as it was always intended to. Whilst the band might have liked more commercial success (not necessarily equating that with a trivialisation of their music – as Howard said in 1977, "You can be on billboards and still go straight to people's hearts") the band remain proud of what they have achieved. As Dorian Lynskey wrote in *Q* magazine in January 2009, "Their commercial failure seems not just unjust but irrelevant when you consider how snarlingly vital their best work sounds today." It seems that Dave Formula's positive assertion through the years of "It will out!" in reference to Magazine's music, is finally fulfilling its prophecy.

Chapter Two —

They don't know how we rehearse our dreams …

The Band

THE DEFINITIVE Magazine line-up of the late 1970s comprised Howard Devoto, Barry Adamson, John McGeoch, Dave Formula and John Doyle. The core of the band either grew up in or had connections with the city of Manchester but each brought different influences and experiences to bear on Magazine's sound. During the lifetime of the band, other musicians came and went and made a contribution to the band's recorded and live output.

Two original members of the group were drummer Martin Jackson and keyboard player Bob Dickinson. Martin was born in Manchester on 30 August 1955. Although his parents were not musical, his older brother and sister were responsible for much of Martin's early music listening. Sleeping above their rooms and hearing them play their collection of Beatles, Nina Simone, Herb Albert and other 1960s pop classics is an early memory. Martin says, "I took up drums, because everyone else I knew had the other instruments, so I kind of fell into drums, rather than choosing them. Music was what I was driven to do."

Starting out as a Beach Boys fan around the age of seven, Martin progressed to exploring the music of Fleetwood Mac, Hendrix, Cream and Dylan. However he says, "The real turning point for me came with the discovery of the MC5 and The Stooges on import, which then led me to the New York Dolls. Their gig at Leeds University was a very influential moment. I then got into Bowie and early Roxy Music and then into Can – whose drummer Jaki Liebezeit was a big influence." Whilst still at school and doing A Levels Martin started recording and playing with The Freshies; the track *Washed Up* (later released as part of an EP) was recorded in Martin's bedroom. He also played in a funk and soul band called Essence, who opened his ears to the music of Sly Stone, Isaac Hayes and dub, and later still, he played in a rock band called 8.5.

Although Bob Dickinson played just three gigs with Magazine, his legacy lives on in the contributions he made to some of their early tracks. Bob was born on 12 June 1955 and was raised in Bury, Greater Manchester. From an early age he was interested in exploring how sounds were produced and manipulated and was unafraid to push the boundaries of what could be achieved experimentally. A continually enquiring mind led him to pursue different avenues around his music making. Around the age of eleven he began to learn to play the violin (and later, the piano) and became interested in not only how violins were constructed but the whole genre of medieval music.

In his teens, whilst his friends were immersed in the world of progressive rock and attending King Crimson concerts, Bob was listening to classical and experimental music. He describes Wagner as being "the first music I listened to which sent shivers down my spine". Hearing Polish composer Krystoff Penderecki's concerto for cello and orchestra on Radio Three opened his ears to the possibilities of avant-garde music. Inspired by John Cage's use of chance techniques to write music, he made his first foray into the world of avant-garde composing by throwing a pin randomly at a piece of white paper and marking the places where it fell.

In 1973, Bob went to Sheffield University to study music, and more specifically composition. With the help of a grant from Yorkshire Arts, Bob set up a new music co-operative, putting on pieces by now internationally renowned artists such as Terry Riley and Philip Glass. The three members of Sheffield-based band Cabaret Voltaire were frequent visitors to the university's electronic music studio and Bob became friendly with them collaborating with them on various multimedia arts events. Around the same time, at the behest of Dick Witts – later of The Passage and an influential figure in Bob's early musical career – he wrote a piece for the International Festival of Mixed Media in Ghent.

Bob was always at his most comfortable when composing and admits he often felt uneasy working with other musicians. He reflects, "I'm working in this classical music area but I never felt comfortable with classical musicians. I never really felt comfortable with rock musicians either – even when I was working with Cabaret Voltaire, it was very much like an anthropologist observing these other people – I'm taking part in this strange ritual but as an outsider, never getting fully involved. I think that's why I did the composition."

Bob went on to do a doctorate at Keele University looking at spatial aspects of electronic music. At the same time he was working on various projects with Dick Witts. In July 1977, they did a five hour performance together at Peterloo Gallery, Manchester – based on a piece of experimental music by Gavin Bryars (and released a year earlier by Brian Eno) called *The Sinking of the Titanic*. It was at this point that Bob had his first exposure to punk rock, as Dick Witts – despite being a percussionist whose CV included working with the world renowned Hallé Orchestra – was a fan. By this time, the Manchester Musicians Collective was under way and held regular meetings in the basement at North-West Arts and musicians from all genres – including fledgling punk bands like The Fall – found themselves under the same roof.

With Bob's background listening to, composing and playing classical and avant-garde music, punk rock seemed an unlikely 'next step'. Apart from Brian Eno's *Another Green World* and the experimental end of The Velvet Underground – especially the chord mantra of *Sister Ray* – rock music in general had had little impact on his musical development. Having been introduced to the music of The Clash and The Fall however, Bob began to make connections between the simplicity and rawness of what he was hearing, and the music of John Cage and the experimental minimal music he was producing. He says, "I wasn't coming to punk through a rebellion point of view, I was coming at it very much from having an interest in minimalist music. Part of my research at Keele looked at the music of Alvin Lucier – incredibly simple music – anybody could do it. This is what punk was about – it was 'do it yourself'. That's what appealed to me about it."

Paul Spencer and Robin Simon both had brief stints in the band playing drums and guitar respectively. Paul was born in Clacton-on-Sea on 13 July 1955. From a showbusiness family (his father was a magician and his aunts ran a dancing school and sang cabaret), he decided quite early on he wanted to become a drummer. Pirate radio held a particular fascination for him growing up, as Radio Caroline periodically broadcast just off the coast near Clacton. On leaving school, he took a job with a shipping company and played in a lot of "very uncool bands" learning how to make a living as a drummer. It was whilst he was playing in a Birmingham show band that the chance came to play with Magazine as a replacement for Martin Jackson.

Robin (né Robert) Simon was born on 12 July 1956 in Halifax and has an older brother Paul who has also followed a musical path. The first gig he attended was Pink Floyd at Leeds Town Hall and he counts among his early influences Captain Beefheart, The Velvet Underground, David Bowie (Mick Ronson era), Neil Young, the MC5 and Robert Fripp. He says, "I was particularly inspired by meeting Ian Dury when he visited Halifax with Kilburn and The High Roads." Later influences included Television, the Ramones, the Sex Pistols, Roxy Music, Gary Numan and, of course, Magazine and Ultravox.

Both Robin and his brother began their careers in music forming bands in their hometown – bands who included amongst their number Billie Currie, later to join Robin in Ultravox. The brothers toured the UK with Limmie Funk Limited but in 1976, they found themselves in London, at the heart of the punk scene around The Roxy Club and The Vortex. Together with Ian North and Martin Gordon (Sparks) they formed Radio, later renamed Neo. In 1978, Robin joined Ultravox, leaving along with John Foxx during their 1979 American tour. He remained in New York, returning to England in 1980 to take his position in Magazine as replacement guitarist for John McGeoch.

Ben Mandelson also took up the mantle of guitar player with Magazine, for their fourth studio album *Magic, Murder And The Weather*. Ben was born in the Everton area of Liverpool on 6 October 1953. His dad played drums at university and he grew up in a family which derived great pleasure from music, but wasn't musical in a way which Ben feels was relevant to his later career. Ben's older cousin – Sydney Torch – was a famous cinema organist before the war and gained further recognition as a band leader on the BBC flagship programme of the 1950s and 1960s – *Friday Night is Music Night*.

Whilst Ben was at school he had piano lessons but perhaps lacking the attentiveness to detail required to understand the disciplines of music at the time, he was not particularly successful in this area. Ben developed an interest in African music from an early age – an interest which has inspired him and sustained him throughout his musical career. Hearing Congolese guitar player Mwenda Jean Bosco (recorded by seminal African record producer Hugh Tracey), on the BBC, was an early influence. Although few of his friends shared this interest, Ben began playing guitar and actively seeking out 'African feel' music.

On leaving school, Ben began a psychology course at Bolton Institute of Technology, which is where he first came into contact with Howard Devoto. He recalls, "Howard and I were new boys on the same day and became very pally. We did lots of artistic things together – made up pretend magazines, enjoyed music together and just generally hung out. We might have made some noise together – sort of squeaking – and got in with the same crowd." Ben's interest was very much what he describes as "avant-garde, hard-core folk and free jazz". He introduced Howard to these genres and particularly what is now generally termed 'world music'. Howard enthuses, "Ben is absolutely the top at that – he knew world music backwards before most people knew where Africa was on the map."

Ben continued to play guitar in a variety of folk orientated groups and fuelled his musical passion by travelling down to London on the overnight bus to attend concerts and spending his grant money on music and secondhand books. Abandoning his college course mid term, he returned to Liverpool and continued playing in bands – one of which became Amazorblades who signed a record deal with Chiswick Records. By 1977, Ben was based in London and touring constantly and punk rock was becoming part of the musical landscape. Although Ben was not part of that scene he recalls, "I was a bit curious – and it encouraged us to play faster and louder. That was fine – I liked the attitude."

In vogue with the times Amazorblades spawned a power pop offspring in the shape of The Blades – "basically us as a quartet but with short hair and matching shirts – very cute". After this band had run its course however, Ben partook in a series of "weird little day jobs" finally earning some money by playing in a theatre band with Ray Burnside. This enabled him in late 1980 to take himself and his fiddle off to the States to discover the world of American music. It was as he returned from this trip that he discovered that his old friend Howard and his by now well established band Magazine were without a guitarist as they prepared to record their fourth studio album. The timing was fortuitous.

Original and definitive Magazine guitarist John Alexander McGeoch was born in Greenock, Scotland on 25 August 1955. He and his younger brother Bill were born into a household that revolved around music – especially orchestral and dance music. John looked up to his father who played piano accordion and he would often go and watch his uncles play in their dance band. John and his brother had piano lessons and Bill was in fact first to take to the guitar at around seven years of age. John started playing guitar after receiving one as a twelfth birthday present and had private tuition playing mainly classical music. John's family remember him as being shy about his talent and performing in front of others although he did eventually make his stage debut playing *Edelweiss* on acoustic guitar at the school Christmas party.

When he was fourteen, John saved up and bought his first electric guitar – a Commodore for £25. (John was still using this at the time of the first Magazine gigs.) Speaking to journalist Lynden Barber in 1980 in an article named *The Correct Use Of Vinyl (International Musician)* John said, "When I was fifteen or sixteen I used to listen to Hendrix and learn his stuff. As a result of that I'm very conscious of not playing standard rock 'n' roll licks, I don't allow myself to do that. But it's almost gone the other way, a humorous thing; I like sticking in rock 'n' roll things just as a joke. I don't like blues-style guitar playing simply because everybody does it. I do work out solos, I don't indulge, I try and write them as melodies almost, not as exhibitions of how good I am at playing guitar."

John played for a while with local outfit 2D Sparklers (later known as the Slugband), performing the hits of the day and covers of Free and Cream classics. At the age of sixteen however he moved with his family to Essex where John attended College. Friend Joe Barry remembers, "I met him on a bus. We were both at Redbridge Technical College. He looked quite striking because he had quite long hair – very colourful looking. We were all kind of hippies then." Joe remembers mutual friend Ciaran Harte as being a big influence on John's playing – along with guitar teacher Mark Knopfler who "pushed on John's technical ability".

John moved on to do an art foundation course at Thurrock whilst earning some money working at the local psychiatric hospital. Joe says, "By this time we'd all moved from being a bit hippy to being a motorcycle group. We all had bikes although John's bike always seemed to be off the road. John was into martial arts – he had a slightly machismo edge to him." His interest in and talent for art then led him to take up a course at Manchester Polytechnic studying fine art. The move coincided with the emergence of punk rock as a musical and social force and John totally immersed himself in the city and its culture. John moved into a flat in student land sharing his space with Malcolm Garrett who himself was studying at Manchester Polytechnic. The social circles that he was moving in meant that it was inevitable that his path would soon cross with that of Howard Devoto.

Barry Adamson was born in Hulme, Manchester on 11 June 1958 and grew up in the neighbouring area of Moss Side. His sister was nine years older so to Barry it felt like he was growing up in a house full of adults. His dad was a very keen jazz fan, but didn't play – unlike his own father who could pick up any instrument and play. Barry says, "For some reason I took that as a bit of a challenge. It was something I could be that my father would respect – something he couldn't do himself. I guess I took that mantle".

Barry's first instrument was a set of claves – a percussion instrument that he'd first heard on the Elvis Presley record *It's Now Or Never*. He says, "My dad heard me listening to it and pointed out this really odd little rhythm amongst the whole thing. The sentiment of the song for some reason really resonated. He was a woodsman at a company that made huge barrels for cable. He carved out a set of claves and brought them home one day – they even had the same tone! I really thought I was destined to be a percussionist or drummer then. I was obsessed with getting a black shiny Premier kit – I even carried the brochure around in my back pocket. I had a set of pots and pans and I could play the drum solo from the Jet Harris and Tony Meehan song *Diamonds* which I'd solely learned to impress my parents in the hope that they would buy me a kit. Which never happened – but funnily enough I have the reissued 1974 black sparkly Premier kit in my studio now!"

A record that was a big influence on Barry was *Late Spot at Scott's* by the Tubby Hayes Quintet. He says, "It just pulled me in – it was jazz but it was British so I could relate to it." Something else that he could relate to was his sister's obsession with all things pop – she was a big fan of The Beatles and The Rolling Stones along with the burgeoning Tamla Motown scene. He says, "All the time I was tuned into what my family were listening to – I hadn't really found anything of my own yet." As a young teenager growing up, Moss Side felt like a great place to be. He says, "In those days there was music pumping out from the basements and shebeens. As a youngster it felt great being able to go into these shebeens and dance through the night listening to all this great music."

At the same time he was going to concerts at the Free Trade Hall (David Bowie, the Groundhogs, Hawkwind) and attended his first outdoor music event. He recalls, "When I was thirteen or fourteen, I went to a festival in Buxton. At the time I was incredibly impressed by The Alex Harvey Band. They looked odd for a start because of what they were wearing and the guitarist had white clown makeup. They played this sort of blues but it had an edge to it. I remember them doing this song – *Framed* – and it had a classic jazz phrase. That was the only thing I can remember apart from the weather was terrible and me and my mates slept in a ditch and got trodden on by Hells Angels!"

Growing up as a mixed race child Barry felt a certain sense of displacement, which was compounded by the way he viewed the world. He says, "I wore it a bit like an alienation badge of honour – being an outsider and therefore being able to plug into outsider things. It was fantastic being able to read Sartre and say, 'I get it'." He continues, "It was different for me, as a mixed race teenager, to be into 'white rock' but I kind of understood what was going on. There's a sense of alienation in that kind of music anyway. I'd sit at home waiting for Alice Cooper imports to arrive from America. The hidden terror, alienation and loneliness, along with the drunkenness and haphazardness, was what I tapped into."

Barry had a couple of violin lessons at school but a combination of a square jaw and a less than sympathetic science teacher (whose lessons he was missing) put paid to any further advancement. At around fifteen, he finally got his first guitar as he explains, "I watched *Top of the Pops* obsessively and tuned into who was playing which make of guitar or bass. I was crazy about the record *Radar Love* by Golden Earring. The guitarist had a Dan Armstrong plexiglass guitar and I told my parents, 'Please – I need – I must have that guitar'. I think they bought it for my birthday."

The guitar lasted little longer than the violin, as Barry was put off when he couldn't immediately play the instrument well. Although his schooling was still full of musical and artistic connections a career in music seemed unlikely. He took art at A level and seemed destined to be a graphic designer – with an interest in designing record sleeves. The baking hot summer of 1976 saw Barry at Technical College doing Art and Design, but also being exposed to and excited by the music of Buzzcocks, The Damned and The Clash – all of whose concerts he attended. He recalls seeing Buzzcocks play at the Lesser Free Trade Hall and says, "Suddenly I'd gone from seeing Led Zeppelin in a huge environment to standing at the bar next to the Buzzcocks and them walking on stage and playing their set. I was completely blown away and I felt I understood every nuance, every tick, everything."

Dave Formula (né Tomlinson) was born in Whalley Range, Manchester on 11 August 1946. He grew up in a musical family; his Grandmother sang contralto at concert parties in the 1920s and 1930s whilst his father, who worked for the gas board by day, was a pianist and semi professional musician by night. Dave recalls that when he wasn't out playing with dance bands in and around Manchester he would play every evening in the family home. The radio formed a backdrop to family life and relayed the popular music of the period – a strange mix of pre-rock 'n' roll standards (Perry Como and George Shearing) and early pop music (The Shadows, The Beatles).

In common with many youngsters growing up in the pre-television era Dave had piano lessons from around the age of nine – at the home of a woman who lived nearby and taught both piano and accordion. Dave remembers his tutor as having a creative approach to her teaching, making use of popular music to keep her young pupils interested and being careful not to put them off with too much theory. The first band Dave saw live was The Shadows, whilst his interest in jazz was nurtured by trips with his dad to see Duke Ellington and Count Basie play at the Free Trade Hall. Along with his musical aspirations, Dave developed a love of theatre and as a teenager joined a youth theatre in the city, throwing himself into a variety of roles, including Shakespeare.

At the same time Dave was mixing with a different set of friends and he was beginning to feel some of the excitement engendered by the early strains of the 'Mersey Beat' drifting across from Liverpool. His desire to play music was heightened by his experience of sitting in with the band attached to the theatre company – playing at the Saturday night dance socials. Inspired, he and his friend Tony Cassidy decided to put together a band for a show they were both appearing in. Perhaps partly due to the moniker they attached to themselves – The Satanists – they attracted some unexpected early press coverage. A review in the *Manchester Evening News* (referring to the traumatised youngsters in the audience and associating The Satanists with the new, unfamiliar music) ran the headline: 'Toy Soldiers retreat – it's the Mersey Sound!'

Dave left school at sixteen and, along with the other 'Satanists', took up a series of casual jobs to support himself. Time spent playing in more commercial bands earned them all enough money to be able to concentrate on developing the musical identity of their own group. Thus The Satanists became St Louis Union and Dave had his first taste of musical recognition. An RnB soul group, St Louis Union first came to widespread attention when they won the *Melody Maker* National Beat Contest in 1965. (Unknowns Pink Floyd were unplaced.) By all accounts the evening was a riotous affair, but St Louis Union emerged with an enhanced reputation, a Decca recording contract, an appearance on popular TV programme *Thank Your Lucky Stars,* a Hammond Organ and lots of new clothes.

St Louis Union's success continued with an appearance in the film *The Ghost Goes Gear* alongside such luminaries as The Spencer Davies Group. They were a popular act, particularly in the Manchester area, and were virtually the house band at The Twisted Wheel beat club. They became part of the mod soul scene and were contemporaries of The Animals, Long John Baldry and a young Rod Stewart (with whom they played when a member of his band, The Soul Agents, fell ill) – and they played four dates supporting Otis Redding.

It was possibly a wrong tactical move on the part of their agents Kennedy Street Artists that inadvertently put paid to a promising career. The real musical identity of the young band was compromised when they were persuaded to cover the Beatles' song *Girl*. Despite this leading to TV appearances on *Top of the Pops* and *Thank Your Lucky Stars* and a chart 'hit', it was the B-side cover, *Respect* (Otis Redding), that gave more of a clue as to the band's influences and ambitions. As Dave muses now, "In a way that decision really killed it for us. We were too naïve." Although other singles were recorded – including a Bob Seger song, which apparently has become something of a cult classic in America – the band never recovered and by the age of twenty, Dave began to think that his pop career was over.

Dave fell back into a series of musical odd jobs and led a fairly soulless existence feeling that he was destined to be nothing more than a musical journeyman. For a year he worked for the Mecca organisation at Tiffany's playing a series of covers amongst the fake palm trees. Then despite his previous less than positive experience he renewed his links with Kennedy Street Artists, forming a four-piece band that the agency used to back different artists. A highlight of this period was being asked to play with Jimmy Ruffin. Rubbing shoulders – albeit briefly – with one of the leading exponents of soul music and having a small connection with the world of Tamla Motown was inspirational.

An involvement with Strawberry Studios in Stockport, eventual home of 10cc, came next. This was followed by stints playing keyboards for different projects before finally settling down for a period with the band Ankh (Egyptian symbol of life). Then, in 1974, Dave was offered a job playing in the band with the musical *Hair*. He travelled to Portugal and Spain with his Fender Rhodes piano, checking it in at customs under his own steam. His father's serious illness however led to him returning once more to Britain.

In a way the subsequent death of Dave's father acted as a spur for what followed. Determined to refocus and get his career back on track, he joined a band called Giro – in Dave's words "almost a pre-punk band" – featuring the vocals of Paul Young, who later had some fame with the band Sad Café. From the rougher side of the tracks, Giro played a mixture of Dr John, The Meters and Bob Marley. They had an anarchic quality to their music and in their approach to playing and their inbuilt gang mentality was liberating for Dave. At the same time, he was listening to a lot of jazz – including musicians like Miles Davies, Joe Zawinul, Chick Corea and Herbie Hancock – along with the hugely inspirational Sly and the Family Stone.

Although music was experiencing a bit of a lull around this time a small scene was developing in Manchester in which CP Lee was a key figure. CP Lee played initially in a band called Greasy Bear – a sort of Manchester version of Mothers of Invention. Later CP Lee took this one stage further with the parody band Alberto y Lost Trios Paranoias on one of whose albums Dave played keyboards. Tellingly, Martin Hannett was mixing in the same social circles, ostensibly as a bass player, and it was around this time that Dave first came into contact with him. An unlikely episode followed whereby both men accepted the offer of a week's work as backing musicians to the cabaret act Faith Brown. As an inexperienced bass player Martin struggled and the rudeness with which he was met by his employers led to the pair walking out and no doubt cemented their friendship. The awfulness of this period was probably matched only by Dave's stint working in a holiday camp – where he was sacked for being a subversive influence!

Meanwhile the band Giro, which was to have been Dave's lifeline, imploded in a sea of volatility. Fortunately it was by now 1976 and punk was on the horizon. Dave was intrigued by adverts for the Sex Pistols, and bands started to come up to Manchester flying under the banner of punk rock. Dave spent time in venues like Rafters taking photos of early gigs. Sham 69 was one of the first punk bands he saw – the audience fascinated him much more than the band and he began to feel some of the intrinsic excitement and sense of a movement. His friendship with Martin Hannett, who was by now producing bands, meant that he was one of the first people to hear the raw recordings of Buzzcocks. Martin sent him Buzzcocks' *Spiral Scratch* along with a recording by Manchester band Slaughter and the Dogs, seeking Dave's opinion on the merit of the two bands. He chose Buzzcocks.

However Dave says of punk, "Although I could see the excitement and the intensity of it and the regeneration qualities of it I actually thought most of the music was pretty poor – it was just too basic for me. I could see why it worked but I can't say I liked the music that much – particularly in the early stages." Nevertheless, he was interested enough to watch when Martin called him and alerted him to the fact that the third gig of new band Magazine was being televised that night. Martin explained that they weren't 'punk' – but that there were 'connections' – and they were looking for a keyboard player.

John Doyle was born on 6 May 1959 and grew up in Denton, Greater Manchester. He and his older brother were encouraged to learn piano – although as John recalls, he didn't share the same enthusiasm as his brother and gave it up after a few years. Attending local public school William Hulme Grammar however meant that music and drama were always on the agenda and a couple of years after starting that school John acquired his first drum kit and formed his first band. Self-taught, John's interest in drumming was sparked by listening to groups like Free and Atomic Rooster. John admits that they never actually got out of practising in the upper hall – and that his band's exploits almost caused its members to be expelled. He recalls, "We were there one Saturday morning, making a hell of a racket, and the school bursar who lived on the grounds came storming up. Unfortunately we were smoking as well, so it was a double whammy – we nearly got thrown out!"

John however was hooked and it was when he started to meet up with likeminded people a couple of years older than himself at a local pub that he got together with his next band. This band made more headway and started to rehearse at a pub near Belle Vue called The Midland. Performing covers on the pub circuit they went by a variety of names – the most memorable being Blue Angel, which as John jokes now, "sounds like a toilet cleaner." It was whilst playing in this band that John realised that he wanted to get more involved in playing the kind of music he was listening to.

In common with other members of Magazine, Alice Cooper was an early influence. John was impressed by the construction of the songs and the sense of theatre. He recalls, "Then the DJ Johnnie Walker introduced me to Steely Dan. There was a progression then to listening to music that was more music orientated – Little Feat – that kind of ilk – that I would consider funky. It was always the drums that caught my attention."

One of the first gigs John attended was Genesis at the Free Trade Hall (one of John's regrets is that he never got to play there). With friends he would enjoy seeing bands such as Man, Budgie and Little Feat at local venues, but was less interested in the likes of Barclay James Harvest and rockier bands such as Led Zeppelin. Later, John became a massive fan of Prince stating, "Rhythmically he is outstanding and the construction of the songs totally amazing. Every beat and every hole just sits, perfectly. I don't care if you like the music or not you can't fault the musicianship."

After the pub band he decided to join something that was more "self penned" and he became a member of Idiot Rouge. John recalls, "Another guy joined at the same time – he was a songwriter in the Graham Parker/Elvis Costello mould writing brusque, brittle songs." Idiot Rouge wore drainpipes and delivered short, sharp songs with a social message. John combined playing in this band with his day job at the insurance firm for which his brother worked. He believed in the songs they were writing but didn't seriously think his future lay in the music world – "that was something that happened to other people". Fate intervened however the night Idiot Rouge took to the stage for what was to be their final gig before other band members put their musical ambitions on hold and went off to University. The gig was the Fresher's Ball at Manchester Polytechnic in October 1978. John McGeoch, ex-student at Manchester Poly and guitarist with Magazine was in the audience. And Magazine were in need of a drummer.

Howard Devoto (né Trafford), who has one younger sister, was born in Scunthorpe on 15 March 1952. Two years later, his father's job (legal and accounting for an oil company) necessitated a family move to Nuneaton, followed by relocation to Leeds in 1962. Howard describes his family's circumstances as being comfortably off.

According to Howard his family were not particularly musical. A delve into the archives by a family member threw up nothing more interesting than a "philandering violinist in the Hull area" on his father's side. Howard's father claimed he could play piano by ear and indulged in some 'boogie-woogie' style playing. The family invested in a piano in 1960 so Howard could have piano lessons; these he kept up until the age of around fifteen and although he enjoyed playing he admits he "never really sparkled at it". A family acquisition of some importance however was their first portable stereo record player. Howard remembers this came as a package deal with a small collection of EPs – a mixed bag of Kenneth McKellar, Hawaiian guitar music and the mandatory "screechy lady".

The first record he ever owned was a present for his ninth birthday. Howard relates the story: "It was my choice so I was taken down to the local record shop in Nuneaton by my mother and given the run of the racks. Not for an album – no no no no – and I don't think we knew about singles. They were behind the counter. It was EPs really – that's what we got with the record player – so that was what we knew about. Initially I picked a Duane Eddy one. I didn't like it much so we took it back to exchange for a Shadows one. I knew the singles, but remember – we weren't looking at the singles. I chose The Shadows' first EP, which didn't have any of the singles on. I got it home and it was one of the handful of very significant moments in my life. I remember thinking 'Oh – this is how life is supposed to feel. When I listen to this – this is how life is supposed to feel'."

Although exposed to the pop music of the time sung by artists such as Adam Faith and Billy Fury, Howard's preference was for bands that had a slightly moody, subversive element to them – hence his preference for The Rolling Stones over The Beatles. His dad took him to his first gig in 1963 to see Jet Harris and Tony Meehan who held more of an attraction for Howard than the clean-cut headliners, Gerry and The Pacemakers. To Howard's great disappointment however, Jet didn't turn up – alcohol abuse having already taken its toll – and instead it was The Tony Meehan Combo (including John Paul Jones, later of Led Zeppelin). Apparently there was a lot of discussion in the press at the time about audiences being paid to scream to create a scene – Howard's overriding memory was of his dad craning his neck during the concert to see if the screaming was genuine or this was indeed true. Howard jokingly blames his continuing problem with the hearing in his right ear on his attendance at an equally high decibel concert in his teens when together with his friends, he went to see The Nice at Harrogate Opera House, supported by Yes.

Whilst Howard was at Leeds Grammar School, he got a band together with his friends, including Richard Boon who went on to manage Buzzcocks. Deeply alienated from school it was only in his later years there that he met some people with whom he felt he had a connection. The Earnest Band was a play on the headmaster's name and only actually played one gig – the Christmas Dance at school. Howard describes the band as a very amateurish Bonzo Dog Doo-Dah Band sort of thing. Although dismissing it now, at the time Howard felt the band had some worth, going so far as to send a tape (recorded on his reel-to-reel tape recorder) to influential Radio One DJ John Peel. Peel responded by means of a Dandelion Records postcard with the words: "Makes a change from all that pseudo revolutionary stuff".

It was around this point that according to Howard "testosterone kicked into my existential confusion". Or to put it more simply, in his mum's words to Howard, "You went haywire!" Although, according to Howard, he was "mediocre" at school, he began writing poetry, even winning a few school prizes for his work. His discovery of Bob Dylan in the summer of 1965 was a contributory factor, as was the influence of an inspirational English teacher who introduced him to the work of Dylan Thomas and Gerard Manley Hopkins. One line from Howard's early poems surfaced later as a lyric in a Shelley – Devoto song: "He cries 'til the stars in his eyes are dead".

Unsure of what direction to take, Howard did a few "musical bits" with Richard Famous (later of the Poison Girls), writing a few songs and putting on one or two performances in Leeds. Equally he was toying with the idea of being a writer. Less than spectacular A Level results meant that offers didn't fall into his lap as easily as they might have done so he took a year out after school and worked in a record shop in Leeds. It was during his time there that he 'discovered' David Bowie when Hunky Dory arrived in 1971. Noticing the reference to Bob Dylan and Andy Warhol on the back, Howard borrowed the album and was hooked. He remembers however that for him, Bowie disappointed as a live performer – having seen him play St George's Hall in Bradford in June 1972. Conversely Alice Cooper as a live spectacle was something that Howard couldn't resist – the previous year he had travelled down to London to see him perform. He remembers, "I enjoyed that gig immensely. Musically they were a bit sub heavy rock but at that time they did seem genuinely radical. When you're that age it's important to have your niche artists. 'They're mine, I'm really into this – you're not? Oh dear ...'"

In the summer of 1972 Howard applied to do psychology at Bolton Institute of Technology. This he did for just over a year and a half then "flaked out". Once more Howard took time out then returned to Bolton to start a new Humanities course in the autumn of 1974. By the following summer, Howard was still on the course but had "had enough of the delights of Bolton" so moved out to live in Salford. He found a place in a house on Lower Broughton Road, owned by one of the tutors. Howard remembers his reasoning at the time: "Manchester was the nearest big city to me. Also this household was quite attractive to me – I was a bit in love with a girl in this household so I was quite anxious to move in – she'd moved out by the time I moved in!"

It was around this time that Howard was listening heavily to The Velvet Underground and The Stooges' album *Fun House* – but also music from a wide range of genres. Classical music remained an interest (Bruckner's *8th Symphony*, Wagner's *Ring Cycle*) and he was introduced to jazz (especially Miles Davies) and world music. He was later to say, "My inspiration for turning to music came from being angrily unhappy. Distressingly so. And from finding that virtually my only company in that distress was The Stooges' records which I played to death when I was at college. And they were so simple – the music was so simple – that I felt that it was at hand to do something similar".

So it was that late in 1975, fed up with the musical diet he was being offered by bands he was seeing at College and in Manchester, Howard placed an advert on the notice board at Bolton Institute of Technology. "I had an idea to form a band," he explained later, "I thought I could do something more exciting." The mention of The Velvet Underground's *Sister Ray* in the advert attracted the attention of fellow student Peter McNeish (later to become Shelley). Howard and Pete began working on some ideas together and practising covers of songs by artists such as The Stooges, Stones and Brian Eno. At the same time, Howard became increasingly involved in the Manchester music scene, putting together gig listings for publications such as the *New Manchester Review.*

But it was reading Neil Spencer's seminal review of the Sex Pistols' Marquee show in the *New Musical Express* (19 February 1976) that set a train of events in motion. Speaking to journalist Kieron Tyler in 2000 Howard remembered, "Pete read it. We were in the refectory at B.I.T. It mentioned they played a Stooges song and said, 'We're not into music, we're into chaos'. At that point we'd been trying for three months, not really getting anywhere, still doing cover versions. Somebody lent me a car that weekend, that's when my life changed."

Howard rang the *NME* to find out where the Pistols were playing and that very weekend, he and Pete travelled down to High Wycombe College of Higher Education – meeting up with friend Richard Boon on the way. They were instantly intrigued by the fact that a few members of the audience (which included such luminaries as Malcolm McLaren and Jordan) almost looked more interesting than the band. Although as Howard noted later in *Sounds:* "Lydon was so charismatic. We thought they were great, the look, the attitude and the music." So captivated were they that they stayed down to attend the Pistols' concert at Welwyn Garden City the following evening.

Howard was determined that the band should come up north to play and spoke to Malcolm McLaren about the possibility of the Pistols playing at the B.I.T. Student Union. When it became clear that this wasn't going to be possible, he managed instead to book the small room above Manchester's Free Trade Hall. Excited to be involved in a real way with an up and coming band that were attracting a lot of attention in the music press, he and Pete busied themselves with arrangements for the gig including the mandatory fly posting to advertise the event.

The Sex Pistols were influential in terms of their music, their attitude and also their dress. Speaking to *Record Collector* in 2000, Howard said, "We immediately changed our look. I started henna-ing my hair, ordered some blue striped jeans and had them taken in." Indirectly, they also led to them finding a name for the band they were putting together; on trawling the London listings in *Time Out* for that Sex Pistols gig they came upon an article for the new TV show *Rock Follies*. The line from the show: "It's a buzz, cock" caught their attention and their band was henceforth known as Buzzcocks.

Around the same time as christening their new band, Howard Trafford and Peter McNeish made the decision to tinker with their own monikers. Thus Howard became Howard Devoto and Peter became Pete Shelley. Howard explains, "It was a name I overheard in conversation at Lower Broughton Road – one of my philosophy lecturers was talking about somebody he knew in Cambridge when he was studying there – a guy who worked on the buses called Andy Devoto, or something like that. I just liked the sound of it. Peter Shelley introduced me, using that name, to probably Caroline Coon or John Ingham – I was a bit undecided up to that point".

With their new identities secured, Howard and Pete prepared Buzzcocks for their first ever gig at the Bolton Institute on 1 April 1976. Howard remembered to Kieron Tyler, "It was the textile students do. I wore knee-length pink boots, my striped jeans, my brown leather jacket. Garth [Davies] was on bass – he and Pete go back a long time. He turned up looking like a cabaret player, in a bow tie, white frilly shirt and a dark suit. We hadn't rehearsed with him at all. Only Pete and I had done anything together. The guy on drums was called Dennis. We had ten songs, most of which were cover versions. *Diamond Dogs*, Eno's *The True Wheel,* probably some Rolling Stones, *I Can't Control Myself* [The Troggs] and a couple of Pete's early songs, *Get On Our Own* and *No Reply*." Despite the fact that as Pete remembered, "We started the second number so fast they couldn't switch us off", the band did get the plug pulled on them after a less than auspicious start, when they inadvertently played *Diamond Dogs* at half the intended speed.

Their second gig was meant to be as support to the Sex Pistols on the first of the Manchester dates (4 June 1976) that Howard had arranged, but the band were still having problems finalising personnel. Although they didn't get to play, it was at this gig that Howard and Pete first came into contact with Steve Diggle. Pete was taking the tickets on the night and remembers, "Malcolm [McLaren] went outside to see if there was anyone hanging around. He'd been out for about ten minutes when he came back in and said, 'Here's your new bass player...' He moved away from the ticket office window and there was a bemused looking Steve Diggle". Steve was invited upstairs to meet Howard and it was only later they discovered that they had got their wires crossed and that he had actually arranged to meet another guitarist outside the venue.

By mid June Buzzcocks had added a drummer to their line up, in the shape of 16-year-old John Maher. John had responded to an advert placed in *Melody Maker* by another musician and it was through contacting her that Howard and Pete got his number and subsequently recruited him. When the Sex

Pistols returned to play the Lesser Free Trade Hall on 20 July 1976, the band were placed on the bottom of the bill. Opening the show, they played to a crowd of around four hundred; a three fold increase in audience size from the Pistols' Manchester debut. Pete remembers, "It was funny because Slaughter and the Dogs tried to hijack it – they had made their own posters which said 'Slaughter and the Dogs plus the Sex Pistols' – and then I think it begrudgingly said, at the bottom, 'plus support.'"

Buzzcocks' next gig was at The Ranch Bar in Dale Street – run by female impersonator Frank Lamar aka Foo-Foo. Considered a 'gay club', the DJs at The Ranch played Iggy Pop, Bowie, Roxy Music, T.Rex and The Andrews Sisters and was, according to Pete, ostensibly an "under-age drinking den - a youth club that served Special Brew!" Pete says, "Foo-Foo was next door in his – or her – Palace performing and tales abound of him coming through the adjoining bar and complaining about the bloody racket! As far as I know, no bands ever played there again!"

The band rehearsed in the basement of the house in Lower Broughton Road where Howard was living. The noise they were making led their next door neighbour to suggest that they moved their rehearsals to the church hall of which he was caretaker. As a thank-you of sorts, Buzzcocks played one 'gig' there. Pete remembers, "There were loads of seven and eight year old kids running around. Howard was getting a bit upset because of all the swear words in the songs. I tried to save the day by suggesting we change the words of *Oh Shit* to *'Oh Spit'* but Howard was still unhappy and there were a lot of songs we couldn't play!"

Buzzcocks played a handful of other gigs in 1976 including providing support at the first ever gig by Eater at Houldsworth Hall on Deansgate. They were determined to play their own music and made a conscious decision not to follow the pub-circuit route. The one exception was a gig at the Commercial Hotel, Stalybridge, which came about through Howard's connections with local promoters. The band played to an audience of bikers and Pete remembers, "We did the first set and it was like oil and water – it was suggested that we leave!"

Immediately after however they travelled down to London, at Malcolm McLaren's request, and played with the Sex Pistols and The Clash at the Screen On The Green in Islington (29 August). Being very early days, there were not yet many bands playing punk rock and Malcolm was keen to have them on the bill. On 21 September, Buzzcocks played the 100 Club Punk Festival, now being joined by acts such as Subway Sect and Siouxsie and The Banshees as well as the Sex Pistols, The Clash and The Damned. Their final gig of 1976 was at the Electric Circus in Manchester in December when they opened once more for the Sex Pistols.

During this period, the band made their first foray into the recording studio, laying down the demos that, although never intended for release, were later to resurface. Howard remembered to Kieron Tyler, "We just wanted to hear ourselves properly. We thought we sounded quite good given how quickly we did it. We didn't have multiple copies. We walked away with two quarter-inches and two cassettes. We hadn't got loads of cassette copies to send off to record companies. It was Pete's copy of the *Time's Up* quarter-inch that he lent to somebody that turned into the bootleg."

In December 1976, having sought the advice of people like Dave Robinson at Stiff Records, Buzzcocks set about recording their first record. Through Howard's connection with the *New Manchester Review* they came up with the producer Martin Hannett and scraped together the money to record the now legendary *Spiral Scratch* EP. Recorded quickly and released on their own New Hormones label it was intended as a snapshot of what was happening at the time. The original pressing of 1,000 records sold out in under a week and by June of the same year sales had exceeded 16,000.

Just as *Spiral Scratch* was released (on 27 January 1977) to favourable media

interest, and when it looked as though Buzzcocks were ready to take the next step up in terms of their musical career, Howard made the decision to leave the band. Pete says, "He was getting a bit frustrated thinking no one was taking it seriously, but he was always doing that. He prefers it when everything's planned out. In fact the line in *Boredom* came from when one day he was complaining that I hadn't done something and I said, 'I don't get round to things, I live a straight line'. We're fundamentally different in that respect."

As Howard left, he cited dissatisfaction with the already tired cliché of punk rock. To the *NME* he said, "I'm tired of noise and short of breath. I'm sick of having to address people out of breath and under my breath." He later clarified his stance issuing the following leaving statement on 21 February 1977: "I don't like most of this new wave music. I don't like music. I don't like movements. Despite all that, things still have to be said. But I am not confident of Buzzcocks' intention to get out of the dry land of new waveness to a place from which these things could be said. What was once unhealthily fresh is now a clean old hat." Still later he elaborated: "Having buggered up one college course, I wanted to try not to bugger up another. I wasn't that wild on punk rock. There was a lot of negative energy, perhaps to its credit. I was uncomfortable, even disturbed, and somewhat scared by some of it. I didn't get my degree anyway."

To reviewers and purveyors of the scene at the time, it was a seemingly momentous decision. Howard himself has always played it down saying, "I don't want any credit for it. I didn't go through any pain making my decision: it happened naturally" (*Sounds* 1977). Nor did he feel trapped in an image or by people's expectations: "At that time I don't think – and I can't think – I had an image to get maternal about. But I'm sure getting trapped in an image can be a big thrill. And expectations are useful things – like deadlines. You only get trapped in them if you let yourself". Speaking to John Robb in 2006 he elaborated, "When I read my leaving statement recently, I thought, 'What did I mean by that?' But I didn't regret it for a moment. People still think I temporarily lost my senses. I still sense this thirty years on, that people can't quite accept why I left."

Although Howard had left Buzzcocks, it was an amicable split and their relationship continued as he explains, "I stayed involved in Buzzcocks, organising gigs, some of the negotiating with United Artists." He travelled down to London to witness Buzzcocks' debut without him at Harlesden's Coliseum on the 11th of March finding it strange initially to hear Pete Shelley singing lead vocals. In fact, Devoto joined Buzzcocks for their encore at the Band on the Wall on the 2nd of May and later accompanied them to London's Vortex on the 4th of July.

Meanwhile he quietly assembled his next band with the intention of recording music which had a little more substance to it than the myriad of copycat bands which had sprung up in the wake of the initial thrust of punk rock. Speaking to *Melody Maker* in January 1978, Howard said, "I was a bit bored with music that went blam-blam-blam. And I was especially bored when I turned round and saw fifty other groups playing music that went blam-blam-blam." The next band was Magazine.

Howard performing with
Buzzcocks at the Electric
Circus, Manchester,
December 1976

Flyer for Buzzcocks 'reunion'
gig at the Lesser Free Trade
Hall, 21 July 1978

Chapter Three —

... on the run to the outside of everything ...

Shot By Both Sides

B Y THE SPRING OF 1977, Howard Devoto's academic commitments were drawing to a close. Although he was still working in a co-managerial role with Buzzcocks, he had more time on his hands and he began to consider the idea of becoming creatively involved with music once again. At the same time, by chance, he was introduced to John Mc-Geoch, a friend of Malcolm Garrett. Howard recalls, "Malcolm mentioned to me that if I was ever looking for any musicians, the guy he shared a flat with was a guitarist and could play all the guitar parts on *Marquee Moon*."

It was at a party at the flat on Wilmslow Road, in April 1977, that Howard and John first met. Speaking in 1980, John recalled, "Punk rock was very young then, and although in London it was about six months older, in Manchester it was still quite a small scene. The only reason I met Howard was because it was a punk party, which was like the thirty punks in Manchester. I was fortunate enough to be one of them."

Howard had continued to collaborate musically with Pete Shelley and songs such as *Shot By Both Sides* and *The Light Pours Out Of Me* had their genesis at these writing sessions. Meanwhile, finding some common ground, Howard and John also began working on some musical ideas together. In the back room at Lower Broughton Road, they continued to work out early versions of these songs plus *Touch And Go* and the 'sandwiches' version of *My Mind Ain't So Open*. The latter song at the time was based around quotations from Samuel Beckett and was a much slower version than the track that eventually surfaced as a B-side to *Shot By Both Sides*.

As John returned home from Manchester Polytechnic for the summer break, Howard began actively seeking out other musicians with whom to collaborate and briefly linked up with guitarist John Scott. At the same time, he placed an advert in Virgin Records in Manchester, wording it carefully so as to screen out people he might not want to meet. As far as Howard's memory allows it went something like this: 'Howard Devoto seeks other musicians to perform and record fast and slow music. Punk mentality not essential. Come woodwind, brass or fire.' Amongst the people who weren't put off by the wording were Barry Adamson, Martin Jackson and Bob Dickinson.

By chance, Barry had just been given a friend's unwanted bass guitar. In possession of only two strings, Barry went into town the following day to purchase some more and spotted the advert in the record store. Immediately aware of the cachet of Howard Devoto, having seen him perform with Buzzcocks at the Lesser Free Trade Hall, he phoned the number on his return home – despite the fact that he had no real musical experience. He says now, "I had an epiphany – like seeing your own destiny in a single moment – and therefore being given somehow the courage to do something you'd never ever do in a million years. It was just a moment where I knew I had to make that call – there was no question."

He continues, "When I got home I got the two strings on. I had no amp but I realised if you leant the neck of the guitar against the bed-head the bed would resonate because it was made of wood. I stayed up all night fooling around and seeing what I could do with it. The next day I went off to Lower Broughton Road." With Howard, Barry ran through a couple of songs including *Shot By Both Sides*. The "otherworldliness" of the song made an immediate impact and Barry was seduced by Howard's ideas, finding himself very much a willing student.

Martin Jackson was also recruited in the same way. He says, "I used to go in Virgin quite a bit and I saw the advert. Punk had a massive impact on me. I followed it right from the days before anything came out. I was into all the New York stuff and bought every single that came out. I'd seen the Buzzcocks a few times at dodgy places like The Ranch and the Electric Circus. I knew other bands like Warsaw and knew Hooky and Ian fairly well, through bumping into them. You'd see the same people at the same gigs."

He continues, "I answered the advert and trundled down to see Howard. I didn't know what to expect but it was clear Howard didn't want to do the same thing as Buzzcocks. I gathered that he wanted a change from 100 mile an hour. We had a chat about music – we both liked Iggy Pop and people like that." For a while during this period it was just Howard, Barry and Martin rehearsing in Martin's parents' house – "in a bedroom with Buzzcocks' equipment and a half broken guitar".

For his part, original keyboard player Bob Dickinson says, "I saw the ad on the notice-board in Virgin, something along the lines of 'New Hormones: if you're interesting then we're interested'. I phoned the number and it was this guy called Howard Devoto, who I'd never heard of (ignorance is bliss in the world of the avant-garde) and we arranged to meet up." Bob went round to Howard's flat in Salford and as he recalls, had an uncomfortable first meeting. He remembers, "When I went to meet him Linder was there with him. I told him I played the violin. He loaned me a book of American poetry and sound poetry, which interested me. (I never gave it him back). He talked about setting Samuel Beckett to music and writing poetry. He was very quiet though and I found the silences really difficult. The atmosphere was as if he was checking you out and I didn't like that feeling."

As John McGeoch came back on board Howard began to consider potential names for his new group. Dave recalls having discussions with him about this at a later date and says, "The main consideration was that it should have more than one meaning. As much as anything it was a reaction against the punk names. With Magazine, I think he liked the literary element and the compendium quality of it alongside the gun association – the edge of violence." Howard concurs, "That did exhibit some appeal – some softness and some hardness, some threat and some leisure," but reveals, "It was kind of triggered by liking Television and going 'that's an everyday object', look round the room, television, bookcase, carpet, curtain, magazine – 'mmm that's got a z in it – that's always zingy.'"

The group began meeting for rehearsals in the basement of a house owned by Paul Roberts in Chorlton. Although small, there was just enough room to rehearse, store equipment and record demos. In a very 1970s detail, Howard remembers the walls of the studio as being lined in denim. It became their base for the remainder of the time the group were in Manchester. The violin was swiftly ditched as it didn't fit in with the overall sound and Bob got himself a Hohner electric piano with wah-wah pedal. Bob describes the rehearsal scenes in the little studio cellar as quite intense. He says, "Howard would be sitting there not saying much, just listening and we'd be playing this mantra of a riff over and over again – then suddenly he'd come in and we'd be hearing words and it was like the sun exploding! It felt special."

Barry felt that the group clicked immediately and was pleased that he was able to make some simple but striking contributions on tracks such as *The Light Pours Out Of Me.* However, he also had an early indication of the way that the balance of creative power was to be distributed as he outlines, "I remember coming up with an idea, complete with title and everything, and I was politely told by Howard, 'Oh – that's not really me.' It kind of made me realise: so this is not going to be a four-way thing or whatever, this is going to be a group name but it's going to be your thing – and I was also aware that things were going to be split up that way too. And I decided then to more or less become a jobbing bass player."

Howard's reputation, built up over the brief but influential time spent with Buzzcocks and his involvement in the early punk scene, meant that there was a lot of media and music business interest in his new band. Martin Jackson recalls, "There was talk at one stage of Tony Wilson managing us and we went to meet him at Granada. He was very enthusiastic but you wondered if any of his ideas would really happen." Demo tapes were sent off to Virgin Records (among others) as early as September 1977 and Andrew Graham-Stewart, who did become the group's first real manager, remembers the excitement they engendered at the time. Simon Draper, head of A&R at Virgin suggested Andrew get involved with the band as Andrew himself explains, "Basically any record company needs to be dealing with somebody who knows their way round the record industry and can get the band going beyond their home town. I went up to their rehearsal space and the relationship developed and I became manager."

Simon Draper was looking to sign bands who had an edge but would also be easier to work with than the unpredictable Sex Pistols who had just been signed to the label. He says, "To me Magazine was absolutely perfect because there was Howard who was a bit of an intellectual and actually wasn't going to be making one chord music for much longer and he was unbelievably hip. I thought they were the perfect antithesis to the Sex Pistols. They weren't quite so dangerous and they had a bit of an intellectual thing to them."

Howard assumed control of the business reigns but says, "The money side of the contract was not heavily promoted – control was what was negotiated." Simon concurs, "Howard was the person I dealt with. He was in charge. I was super anxious to sign them. There were a couple of bands in that era who, not only were very important to me, but were important to the whole company – XTC and Magazine. XTC were absolutely the darlings of the company because Al Clarke – press officer – loved them. While Magazine weren't quite so much fun, they were incredibly supported by the company. And of course that first single, which Mick Glossop produced, made it look like they were going to be huge – it was such a strong single."

"When we were signing Magazine the pitch to them was total artistic freedom. Design your own labels, design your own sleeves – which would have been a major thing for them. Why would you want the record company to interfere with the design when you've got Linder who can do it?" The sense of excitement within the band was palpable and Barry says, "Once *Motorcade* was introduced I thought we were off – we had these amazing songs, got signed, had dinner in a Thai restaurant to celebrate, we had a manager and we had a frontman who continued to do for me what he had done in Buzzcocks, which was to spin this other world."

Having tired of the relentlessness of punk, Howard was trying for something different with Magazine. However, he says, "The master plan isn't all drawn up it just kind of evolves. In some ways Magazine just came together to record *Shot By Both Sides.* I know that when we were talking to Virgin I was thinking: 'This document's talking about all these albums we're going to make – I'm not sure we're going to make all these albums, I'm not sure if we're going to make even one but you seem to think we are and that seems to be the way the thinking in the band's going. We've got a few songs by now so maybe we will'. I was very non-committal in a sense to something that needed a lot of commitment. 'Sure we'll actually finish an album – not sure we're going to tour. Record *Shot By Both Sides?* Yes, we'll do that!'"

Magazine, in fact, played their first gig at the closing night of the Electric Circus in Manchester on 2 October 1977. It was an impromptu performance with equipment borrowed from Buzzcocks. Bob recalls, "It was the first time I'd ever played live at a rock venue. It was very dirty and smelt of drink and pee. I remember seeing Olly from The Worst – out of it in the corridor, condom hanging from pierced ear. John Cooper Clarke played before us and spilt beer on the piano. There was a lot of excitement for Howard's new band – it was a really powerful experience." The band played *Shot By Both Sides, The Light Pours Out Of Me* (introduced by Howard as "This is disco despair – but not the title") and *I Love You, You Big Dummy.*

Magazine's official debut at Rafters followed soon after – a gig that was billed as a benefit for the *New Manchester Review.* Again there was a great deal of anticipation for the band's first full appearance. From the very beginning, Howard was interested in bringing theatrical elements to the performance. He recalls, "It was for that gig that I decided to wear make-up – I think Linder had helped me put it on – and I remember going in to the dressing room and John going, 'Great – we're going to be wearing make-up!'"

An early interest of Howard's was street theatre and the idea of illusion – the philosophical and existential implications of dealing with the fact that you can't believe what you've just seen. He says, "I'd made a suggestion – probably to Andrew Jaspan who ran *New Manchester Review* – that I'd like to have somebody doing illusion type things where they eat glass and swallow gold-fish. That was trying to introduce an element of that. I never even knew he'd got that together until I read one of the reviews that made a passing comment to this hopeless performance. I'm sure it wouldn't have turned out at all like I'd imagined – I think this guy would have just come over as an act from cabaret!"

At this early stage, the band had still to fully flex their song-writing muscles and material for live gigs was limited. Howard recalls, "At Rafters we had a song that was probably only around for that gig – something about shouting legs – running away on my shouting legs. One of the musical ideas from that went into *My Tulpa*. We weren't a band that had been around for years so we didn't have a long repertoire hence my 'I'm not sure we'll even make it to an album'." The set list also included *Shot By Both Sides, Motorcade, Burst, Touch And Go, Peking Hooligan* – and the Iggy Pop song *I Got A Right.*

Jon Savage, who reviewed the gig for *Sounds,* noted that Howard's stage persona was well suited to the lyrical themes of perception, paranoia, and mis-understanding. He wrote of Howard, "He will stare, confront the audience, then back off, eyelids fluttering, to disappear from view under the heads of the front of the audience, to reappear at the start of the next verse. Throughout he moves with the careful balletic grace of a mime artist...hypnotic, haunting, disorientating." To complement this, later, Howard had a special microphone stand built – this he would climb and perch atop, legs wrapped round, eyes confronting the audience.

Magazine's next outing was the specially arranged gig at the Queen Elizabeth Hall, Belle Vue. Over three nights, performances from bands such as The Clash and Steel Pulse, along with Magazine were filmed for transmission on the Granada TV Show *So It Goes* – brainchild of Tony Wilson. Howard knew Tony Wilson very well and says, "He was very supportive of Magazine," adding dryly, "until I had an affair with his wife..." The gig was a slightly bizarre event as Paul Morley recounted in *NME:* "The audience, there by default, appear bemused, confused, reluctantly curious, fascinated – hardly daring to stare straight into frontman Howard Devoto's eyes." More than thirty years later this surreal quality is captured for the YouTube generation as Howard sings *Motorcade* under the crowd's watchful gaze.

The Belle Vue gig was to be the last time Bob Dickinson played with Magazine. He reflects, "I enjoyed being on stage, but I knew that I was having to work harder at it than the others. I was coming from a classical background – I'd never really played with a rock group. I could cope with reading music or free experimental music – but I wasn't a natural rock musician. At the Electric Circus I had my card with the chords on – I needed the security of a score – they didn't need that. I was young, coming from a different tradition and inhibited by the context I was being required to function in."

Although Bob wasn't as comfortable as the rest of the group with their experimentation with fashion and make-up, he was still enjoying the notoriety of being interviewed and photographed for the music press. He was, he says, "buzzing with being in the band". At the same time, however, he was continuing to do side projects with Dick Witts and, more at ease in this world, Bob began to harbour doubts about whether he really fitted in with Magazine. Although he found the other band members to be friendly, warm and open, he wonders in retrospect whether discussions were already taking place behind his back about his future with the group. Nevertheless, after the Belle Vue gig he returned to Keele, where he was still doing his doctorate, feeling very much a part of the band.

It was at this point that Bob received a call asking him to come back up to Manchester for a meeting with all the band members. Bob was informed that the group felt he didn't really fit in. Howard reflects, "He was much more a kind of academic musician – much more into avant-garde kind of classical music. That could have been an interesting angle, and he certainly brought some musical ideas to things, which we went on to use." However, he explains, "He just wasn't built for life on the road. It was kind of – an executive decision has to be made. I must have talked about it with the others but having said that it's such early days with the group. I've pulled the group together and by this point I was a well-known face on the Manchester scene so in truth they're probably going to agree with me. They want this thing, they want to be in a band, they want the record contract. The main man says 'I think this man's gotta go' so he's gotta go..."

At the time Bob remembers he was hurt and upset: "I went back to the rehearsal studio and Howard gave me £70. I wanted what I was due and was a bit pissed off." Now he says, "In retrospect, I think they were right to make that decision. I was coming from a different musical context to them. I don't think they were questioning my musicality. I think they were looking for somebody who could come up with the sounds they wanted and contribute to the arrangements more. When you listen to Dave – fantastic stuff – his pedigree as a rock musician was better than mine. Dave's keyboard parts are very textural – I don't think I could have done that. I don't think I would have wanted to do that."

Without a keyboard player on board, Magazine entered the studio to record debut single *Shot By Both Sides.* Simon Draper engaged the services of Mick Glossop as producer; he was known for his work at Townhouse and had supervised the recordings at the Belle Vue gig. Recorded at Ridge Farm, Mick remembers the sessions as being trouble free. He says, "Although the band were inexperienced, they came well rehearsed and it was a painless operation. I set them up as a band in the studio and they played the track live." As is usual, some parts were then replaced or overdubbed – and the delay on the word 'Shot!' was subsequently changed – but the essence of the track remained as a live performance. Coupled with the reworked *My Mind Ain't So Open* ('punked' up by Martin, John and Barry after a night at the pub) it was released in January 1978. An alternative version, produced by John Wood, later surfaced on the band's box set *Maybe It's Right To Be Nervous Now,* released in 2000.

Speaking of how he wrote *Shot By Both Sides,* Howard says, "I had that phrase from a lesbian woman I was having an affair with – who was also an ardent socialist. We were arguing the toss about something and she said to me 'Oh you – you'll get shot by both sides'. This was in the house at Bolton (living in the room where I bought *Fun House* and first met Peter), before Buzzcocks, before any music and it just went 'ping' – wow, that's like a key phrase!' Obviously at some point it came back to me."

He continues, "After I left Buzzcocks but was helping manage them and doing a little bit of co-writing with Peter, he played me what to him would become the Buzzcocks' song *Lipstick.* All I heard was the riff. I was so enthusiastic about it that he said, 'Okay, I'll give it to you'. So when eventually he released his version I was a little bit pissed off actually. It was a case of – you gave it to me. So it was like two things – I'd got this phrase that went 'ping' and I'd got this guitar riff that really does something for me and I pulled the two together."

Howard revealed just what the song meant to him to John Robb. He says, "I felt a lot about that song when I recorded it. I know when I recorded the vocals it felt like one of the biggest moments of my life. I almost wanted to keep the bit of carpet I was stood on! Lyrically, political commitment was something

I struggled with for many years – I always had the tendency to try and argue the other case and I guess I was trying to sing about what that felt like. Feeling that, you don't always have a lot of certainty about anything. It's not always an easy place to be." Barry recalls his own excitement upon the single's release – he even went to the station himself to pick up the boxes of vinyl because he couldn't wait to see the finished record.

Critics shared the band's enthusiasm and the single was greeted with almost universal acclaim. Described later by *Rolling Stone* as 'the best rock 'n' roll single of the year', it elicited a feverish response from journalists. The *NME* wrote giddily in January, "There's a sweet, desperate, skidding guitar solo which pulls back into the mainline exhilaration, a discreet metamorphosis into a dark, pained, soft section that climbs tightly into a sparkling orgasmic climax before charging back into a repeat of the memorable chorus. The end, hard and sudden. A multi-levelled piece, merging simplicity with complexity." They tagged Magazine as, "The most convincing post-punk band so far. The true inheritors of the mantle of the original Roxy Music."

To promote the single a short tour was organised which would take the band away from their hometown for the first time. Minus a keyboard player there was one further abortive reunion with Bob Dickinson in an attempt to make it work, but essentially Howard was looking for someone who was more experienced. Dave Formula fitted the bill. He gives an example, "I think at one point I was quite keen to use a string machine keyboard which produces orchestral sounds – string sounds. Bob hadn't used one before, didn't have one but managed to borrow one. Whereas you talked to Dave and he'd already used one and he could talk about them. If he didn't exactly have one himself at that point, he knew what he would use if he wanted one – he was a more seasoned musician in terms of pop rock music."

Dave shared a flat with mutual friend Martin Hannett and had seen Magazine play at Rafters. Encouraged by Martin, he watched their performance on *So It Goes* and was further intrigued by their approach and the atmosphere they engendered. Further listening convinced him that the notion of playing in the group was something worth exploring – and so it was that a meeting was arranged between Dave and Howard in a Manchester pub. Having found some common ground and with a feeling that they could work together, ("Linder clocked him and went 'he looks alright'"), Dave began rehearsals with the band at their practice space in Chorlton-cum-Hardy. He then joined the band for what he felt was a trial period of six gigs in early 1978.

At this early stage, Dave was still using his Hammond Organ and Fender Rhodes – instruments that were a hangover from the period he'd just come out of. Referring to the Hammond he recalls, "I knew it didn't look right for the band. I bought a Yamaha organ on tubular steel stands that you could play at rakish angles. I still kept the Leslie speaker – a revolving speaker that gives you

Publicity photos of first line up from 1977
A photo from this session was used on an early promotional flyer (Page 10)
Below: Howard Devoto, Bob Dickinson, Martin Jackson, Barry Adamson, John McGeoch

Howard at Rafters, Manchester, 28 October 1977, and Linder's flyer for the First UK Tour *(below)*

MAGAZINE

24 January
100 CLUB, London

25 January
SANDPIPERS, Nottingham

26 January
RAFTERS, Manchester

27 January
ERICS, Liverpool

30 January
NASHVILLE, London

31 January
BARBARELLAS, Birmingham

1 February
F CLUB, Leeds

Pennine Studio, 26 September 1977
Howard is playing the 'legendary' Woolworth's Starway guitar
also used for a long time by Pete Shelley

Barry Adamson drawing, 100 Club, 24 January 1978

Video shoot, at the Rainbow, 1978

Video shoot, at the Rainbow, 1978

that sort of Hammond sound – I wouldn't let that go! I still kept that – which was part of the Magazine sound. It was more a visual thing, an image thing as much as the sound – the sound was very similar. We were always aware of our image!" He continues, "The Fender Rhodes had to go though as it wasn't right – it was too reminiscent of that jazz rock thing – completely the wrong sound."

A few months prior to joining Magazine, Dave had purchased an ARP Odyssey synthesiser. He remembers, "It didn't have any instructions and I'd never had a synthesiser before. I found it really quite hard initially to get my head round it. I was a little bit lazy with it really. But as soon as I joined Magazine I thought 'This is really going to work' – because of the edginess of the songs they were doing and I really got to grips with it very quickly, because I had to!"

Dave describes the first few days' rehearsal with the band as a "revelation". He says, "McGeoch was so good and Barry, you could see, had this amazing feel. I suppose they thought me coming in was a bit odd – they hadn't really worked with synths before. I think they could hear immediately what they could do with the sound." He elaborates, "Musically – I was really taken by John's approach of breaking musical rules. Some of the changes he'd come up with – the way he'd change a chord and some of the timing things really struck me as something quite original – not incredibly sophisticated musically but it is because it's so different. And the fact that Barry had this funk thing in his playing – that was hitting two areas which really appealed to me immediately."

Up until this point Dave had still been using the surname he'd been born with – Tomlinson. However he says, "It seemed like a new start on joining Magazine. It was kind of fashionable to have strange names. I was driving past a petrol station in Chorlton-cum-Hardy and I just looked up and it said 'New formula petrol'. It had slightly dark elements to it; I realised it was going to be a lot more memorable than Tomlinson."

With Dave Formula on board, Magazine headed to the capital to perform their first London gig – at the 100 Club on 24 January 1978. Although the band were nervous, and the set list limited, they were buoyed by the amount of interest in their first outing with the new line-up. Dave remembers coming back to the venue pre-gig time and seeing a massive queue of people down Oxford Street. He recalls, "It was incredibly exciting to be going out with all this new material. It was edgy as well because the band were still finding their feet. We'd done a lot of rehearsing in Chorlton but to actually go out was a completely different affair."

Writing in *Melody Maker,* Chris Brazier delivered his verdict. He wrote, "Magazine's first ever London gig was An Event from the start." Although feeling that it lacked some of the impact of the band's short set at the Electric Circus a couple of months earlier, he put this down to first night nerves, saying, "Devoto assumed an air of confidence, but he was probably just as scared as his band... this was still a performance of at times startling power." He continued, "It was his group that were mainly responsible for this gig's potency. John McGeoch's guitar gave Magazine its own fiercely original 'spot to stand on'. Or rather run from. What's consistent in their 'sound' is searing guitar lines and weird progressions, which locate their work atmospherically somewhere on the brink."

Much of the press attention around this time however was singularly focused on Howard Devoto. Later dubbed 'The Most Important Man Alive' by the *NME,* early encounters between Howard and journalists had led to the singer being tagged with an intellectual label. This was a state of affairs which was fuelled by Howard's references to works of an existentialist nature and refuelled by journalists appearing to be slightly intimidated and asking questions with an abstract and philosophical bent. Howard looks back with amusement now and laughs, "There was an early Buzzcocks' press release that did so much mischief to my reputation as an intellectual. A lot of it can be traced back – I think – to this press release where I go on about Albert Camus and I think I use the word metanoia – an experience of overwhelming strength that transforms you."

Howard simultaneously fanned the flames and tried to douse them. On the one hand he continued to portray himself as having an intelligence and breadth of interest somewhat beyond the average rock musician, having compared the 'hero' of Buzzcocks' song *Breakdown* to Des Esseintes or Dostoyevsky's underground man before expanding with, "*Breakdown's* hero is in the position of Camus' Sisyphus: 'To will is to stir up paradoxes'." Early interviews flirted with the themes of futility, absurdism, existentialism, sick sensibilities and love.

Conversely, however, he also was at pains to refute the intellectual label. Speaking to Jon Savage in *Sounds* (November 1977) he replied to the suggestion that his lyrics were "above and beyond most punk bands" with, "I'm not interested in being 'beyond' most people: i.e. over their heads. I get vertigo just like the rest. Sometimes it's better just to get under people's feet." Speaking to *Melody Maker* in January 1978, he declared, "Calling me an intellectual is like calling common-sense witchcraft." On being asked if he considered himself an existentialist he replied, "I don't really know what it means. I've read books that are supposed to be of that strain and yeah – I've thought I could go along with it in my weaker moments – but it's not like being a gas-fitter or a clown – is it? There's a little bit of the gas-fitter in me and a little bit of the existentialist."

Some rock journalists were aware of the faintly ridiculous position they had got themselves into in interviews with Howard. In a follow up to an earlier encounter, Chris Brazier in *Melody Maker* wrote, "In a way my interview with him the other week had an atmosphere of absurdity about it. Daunted by his intellectual image, I'd somehow envisaged having to prove my intelligence to him before making any real progress – I ended up sounding insufferably pretentious, coming out so earnestly with questions about the soul, the nature of love, existentialism and that sort of crap. I'd even read Huysmans's *Against Nature* simply because he'd once quoted its 'hero' Des Esseintes as an influence."

Howard initially only wanted to deal with the press in writing in order to retain an element of control over the proceedings. The first half of the 1977 Jon Savage interview in *Sounds* was conducted in this way, but the journalist found it an unsatisfactory experience so against his better judgement, Howard agreed to meet him face to face in a service station café on the M62. Howard admits now that to an extent he was playing games with the journalists and being deliberately obtuse. He says, "I think back then I felt why be bland? I'm just perverse sometimes. Also probably my biggest most consistent musical hero has been Bob Dylan and he absolutely played that far more brilliantly than I ever could in the 60s. His interviews around the time he went electric were just a model of how a modern musician is at the peak of their act."

Some rock journalists and photographers didn't take kindly to what they perceived as Howard's aloofness and arrogance. Howard says, "Some were genuinely pissed off. Chalkie Davies [photographer] was pissed off with me – and I didn't even know I'd done anything to piss him off! This is when Charles Shaar Murray interviewed me for *NME* [February 1978], for the cover story. The interview was carried out in Charles Shaar Murray's hotel room. Chalkie Davies wanted me to do something I did not want to do like stand up on the window ledge or something and I thought, 'No I don't want to stand up on the window ledge,' but I either wasn't supposed to say that – or declined his kind offer in the wrong sort of way."

Charles Shaar Murray unleashed his ire in the piece with a personal attack on Howard, writing, "To me he's that most irritating of human personality types – the infinitely arrogant introvert – the man who illustrates his contempt not by the bellowed insult but by turning his back. During the photo session which followed our interview, he turned out to be the most uncooperative subject I've yet seen in several years of sitting in on photo sessions." In Howard's eyes, Chalkie Davies nurtured his grievance and used it against the singer in subsequent unflattering photo shoots.

From the beginning, Howard railed against what he refers to as "the easy flow of the music business". At the 100 Club gig, questioning the perceived wisdom of how things were arranged, he stipulated that everyone had to pay to get in. There were to be no 'freebies' for journalists and record company people. He reflects now, "I was told that was maybe not too clever, probably by our manager. I was just being an awkward bugger because suddenly I seemed to have a little bit of power." Possibly tongue in cheek, he smiles now, "Yes I do seem to recall passing Simon Draper in the queue outside as we went in..." Andrew Graham-Stewart remembers that this action did not go down very well with the press and possibly adversely affected reviews of the gig. Certainly *Sounds* ran the uncomplimentary headline: 'Animated Egghead fails to impress'. To some extent, the tone had been set.

Following the release of *Shot By Both Sides* and the mini-tour at the beginning of the year, Magazine were invited to appear on *Top of the Pops* to promote the single. Concerned about his credibility and that the mere act of appearing on *Top of the Pops* might be perceived to be a 'sell-out' Howard turned the offer down on behalf of the band. A big factor in his decision was that the bands featured had to mime to their tracks and he was unwilling to go through the pretence.

A week or so later, Magazine were offered the chance to appear again and Howard relented, perhaps realising that it was too good an opportunity to miss. In accordance with Musicians Union rules, the track was rerecorded, in readiness for miming to, but with what Howard describes as a 'deader' vocal. He explains, "The vocal on the single was a bit of a ferocious performance and there was no way I could produce that under miming circumstances – or even *Top of the Pops* studio circumstances. I knew I would not even want to produce the simulation of such a heated vocal in such a naff environment."

As well as an understated vocal, Howard put in a near immobile performance that reflected none of the energy of the recorded – or indeed live – performance of the song. For the *NME* it was a "curiously unimpressive and inexpressive *Top of the Pops* where Devoto appeared too static and sluggish behind rather silly eye make-up". In an almost unprecedented occurrence following an appearance on the hugely influential chart show, the record dropped down the charts the following week.

Although he had sympathy with Howard's principles, Andrew Graham-Stewart felt the band, at this early stage of their career, had made a fatal error. He says, "By the time we did the show, the momentum of the sales had gone. Had it been done at the time it was offered that was the perfect timing and that single would have been much bigger than it was. It would have got higher up the charts and brought in a bigger audience than it did. I think that was a big mistake career wise."

Talking of his relationship with Howard at this time, Andrew says, "He didn't suffer fools gladly. With someone like Howard if you try and push him into doing something that he really doesn't want to do completely against his own ideals then the relationship will just break down. Any manager has to retain the confidence of the artist; if you try and push them into something too overtly commercial a band with principles will just run a mile. I never took a strong line on that. Virgin were used to difficult artists. They had several artists on the roster at that point that could be pretty awkward – in particular the Sex Pistols. Despite everything, most interviews happened and generally the press were looked after."

The *NME* wrote of Howard in February 1978, "He is in the odd position of courting the world via rock and roll – and at the same time punishing it for its shallowness and insensitivity by retreating into reclusion at the slightest provocation." Howard himself says, "My desire was to do things in a different way – if *Top of the Pops* had been a live show that would have been fine. I actually think I was fairly ambitious in those days – I was the one who wanted *Shot By Both Sides* to be more expensive. I remember proposing to Virgin that we should charge a quid – deeply unstreet! And they were 'No way!' whereas they were usually fairly agreeable... I did bloody loads of press – 1978 was the year I did more interviews per square inch of life and more gigs per square inch of raw torn existence than any other year."

Although the rest of the band had been keen to do the television appearance from the off, this was still early days. Despite being disappointed that the record went down they accepted that Howard had his reasons for initially turning down the slot. For Barry, looking back, it was the first sign of Howard attempting to arrest a situation, where he was beginning to feel out of control, with a hint of sabotage.

Howard reveals, "Remember I was the main man and I was pulling as full a part of my own weight as I could at that time. There was a memorable occasion to me when Dave and I were getting a cab back to our homes in Manchester after something or other and the cab driver going – 'Aren't you that Howard Devoto?' and me replying, 'Yes I am and this is my keyboard player Dave.' I got quite an angry response from Dave the next day. I knew I was probably pushing it a little bit but thought maybe I could get away with it... Generally for the first couple of years I had the big voice in how things were done – but not a unilateral one."

With the ecstatic response to *Shot By Both Sides* – despite its relatively low chart placing of 41 – it seemed the band were poised to go on to claim their rightful place in the post-punk chronicles. Almost by chance, Howard had surrounded himself with musicians who were to stand head and shoulders above many of their contemporaries. Although some sections of the press were wary, many journalists and music fans were intrigued by the band and their enigmatic frontman. Writing in *Melody Maker,* Chris Brazier said, "You'll have gathered by now that I find Magazine *very* exciting. I also reckon Devoto will either end up as an Eno-figure dabbling adventurously, intelligently, on the fringe beloved more of writers than of real human beings, or, Bowie-like, towering over trends on the twin pillars of critical and popular response. Either way he won't fail. End of sermon". The stage was indeed set.

Chapter Four —

Everything is where it ought to be …

Real Life

BY THE TIME Magazine entered the studio in early 1978, they had written and rehearsed the tracks that were to make up their debut album *Real Life*. Simon Draper introduced the band to producer John Leckie who was already working with Virgin artists XTC. John was, and still is, a highly respected music producer having started off his career as a tape-operator, then engineer, at Abbey Road working with artists such as John Lennon and George Harrison. He engineered albums for Pink Floyd, amongst others, before going on later in his career to produce influential albums by many bands including The Stone Roses, Radiohead and Muse.

The first track John worked on with Magazine was second single *Touch And Go*. Although the production on the record was praised, the song suffered by comparison to the universally acclaimed debut *Shot By Both Sides*. Additionally, reviewers seemed unsure whether to take B-side *Goldfinger* seriously. As is often the case however, a band's choice of cover material signposts musical influences and John Barry united all the members of Magazine in their admiration of his work. As Howard said at the time, "I like that song very much – and I like the version that we've got together of it. I wanted to do a song from that stable of songs and that one just fitted in very well with what the rest of the songs are about."

Most of the album was recorded at Ridge Farm with further recording and mixing at Abbey Road. At that time, Ridge Farm was a family run place with a rehearsal barn and accommodation in the house. John remembers, "I recorded on the Virgin mobile truck (with a Raindirk desk on Ampex 24 track!), so the control room was outside the barn in the yard." The band were recording there at the time of their inaugural *Top of the Pops* appearance and John recalls with amusement how they almost didn't get to see their debut performance on the show: "Ridge Farm was run by Frank Andrews. I can remember it was Thursday night, 7.30, we'd had dinner early and had to ask Frank to use the TV room. He came back and said 'no' because his Mum was watching the other side! We went back to the studio and sulked a bit, had a few more beers and I went back and pleaded with him. He let us in, his Mum left the room and we saw their bit and left and got back to work. They didn't seem that phased by it and I seem to remember we all just had a good laugh about it."

Musically and lyrically Howard assumed a major role on this album. John recalls, "Although Howard was the quiet one, he would always be there, always in the background. He was an almost silent observer – you sensed he was the unspoken one in control, the figurehead of the whole thing. The rest of the band tried to do everything they could to complement his songs."

In fact, some of the tracks predated Magazine in their conception. *The Light Pours Out Of Me* was initially worked out between Howard and Pete Shelley. Talking about the song, Howard says, "I liked the idea of using the word *pours* about light. Many people didn't pick up on that – some even called the song *The Light Shines Out Of Me*. Because I only had more or less that phrase, Pete just wrote two or three chords behind it – which is the chorus."

It was in early rehearsals with Magazine that the song developed. Howard remembers, "Martin started playing that rhythm and I just said – '*that* – don't forget *that* – keep *that* going!' I came up with those kind of sub Gary Glitter Band things myself and the chorus, but then John came up with what I always think of as the 'shining light' interludes. It just goes – *brilliant* – that's the word *brilliant*! That's what that guitar did – there was the idea of light – and he played something that was light! I've always linked it a little bit to Television's *Guiding Light* from *Marquee Moon*. I always thought – John – that's a little bit of Tom Verlaine – which was a very nice reference to have. A little bit of the sound of *Guiding Light* in a song about light."

He continues, "The other bit of serendipity with it is that the song ends on one of these 'shiny light' bits and it's very abrupt. That's because when we were demoing it, before Dave was in the band, the multi track ran out at that point. But it's perfect – it works! We thought – that take's okay, we don't want to do it again – that's our ending!"

The original keyboard arrangements for the track were the work of Bob Dickinson on an electric piano, with pedal effects. Bob himself describes them as, "suspended chords fading in with slow filtering and pedal repeated Es over the top of the arrangement in the chorus." Dave took it on and says, "What I liked about it was he'd done this kind of swell thing that bloomed out behind it so I just opened it up and used the wah on it. The octave thing was Bob's as well. I thought it worked really well so why change it? I just developed it a little bit. The guitar riff was so strong it filled lots of frequencies – live and recorded there wasn't a lot of room to start piling lots of stuff in it."

Bob Dickinson also wrote the keyboard introduction to *Motorcade* as well as the chord progression, which underpins the whole song. Additionally, influenced by the music of Erik Satie he developed the keyboard counter-melody coming up with a sequence that veered away from a standard chord structure. Howard adds, "John did a fantastic job of augmenting that with all the guitar parts he put over it right through the song." Bob describes the song as "one of the most dissonant and atonal of Magazine's songs" comparing it to The Velvet Underground's *Sister Ray* in the way that it evolves, building into "that manic guitar solo with John McGeoch doing weird scale patterns then going back down and disintegrating into noise."

It didn't occur to Howard that, lyrically, people would go on to assume that the song was about the scene of President Kennedy's assassination. In fact the lyrics were inspired by an article he'd read in a colour supplement a year or two earlier, about a South American dictator who rode around throwing money out of the window to his people. He explains, "The line about 'into the null and void he shoots': in my mind when I was writing it – that was the guy in the motorcade who's as it were driving. Shooting into the null and void of the road ahead – not literally shooting. But it isn't just about that dictator. It's about a mixture of things…. I'm mixing in to it Zen things, the idea that in some ways the most significant decision you can make in your life is whether you're going to drink coffee or tea – however powerful you are. Again, there's the theme of perception – going back to the sword swallower/glass eater. I believe all that I read now – accepting. Just trying to create a scene."

He continues, "The songs with Magazine start to be, a little bit, meditations on power. With Buzzcocks I hadn't written about that I wouldn't say really (perhaps indirectly) but by Magazine that was a big, big thing for me. Because I'd tasted some myself for the first time in my life. Yes there's the fan level thing – but even the thing of the first advance we'd got. £4000 cheque from Virgin. Back on the train to Manchester, down to the bank, the girl behind the counter was 'Hello can I help you? Any more I can do for you?' – where before I'd just been a piece of student scum."

As a lyricist, Howard took inspiration from his personal experiences and his love of literature – references to Huysmans, Camus and Dostoevsky abound along with more obscure works. In common with many songwriters, Howard carried a notebook with him and would jot down ideas and snippets of overheard conversations. He says, "I'd just have a line, maybe three or four lines – the vague shape of something. For some reason I would just be going, 'that's a headline phrase, that's the title of something, that's the chorus of something.'"

Dave recalls, "He always seemed to have a real arsenal of phrases and words and things so you never knew what would come out of it, and you never knew how things had been taken from one set of writings and put together – he didn't talk about those things. He would generally take it away, try a couple of ideas, and come back with it pretty much complete. I can't ever remember him – apart from a couple of occasions– sitting down and saying, 'I haven't got anything for this whole section'. He was very fastidious in the sense that he would have stuff. A lot of the time he'd have his book while you were having a conversation and he'd be jotting down things you were saying."

He laughs, "The most amusing thing was when you could actually remember saying something and he would have picked up on a phrase. You know when you're with a group of friends someone will introduce something and it becomes part of your parlance – part of the way you talk. One that I introduced was 'I can't do that – I've not been very well today'. Of course it's just complete nonsense – just a silly phrase – but that came into one of the songs later on."

Many of the ideas in *My Tulpa* resulted from Howard reading *A Crack In The Cosmic Egg* by Joseph Chilton Pearce. He describes it as a very significant book for him at the time. He says, "I read about this order of Tibetan monks that by some process brought into existence a second being that perhaps might even resemble them. And the idea of producing this was one to play with – a mirror image of you or to be in a relationship with somebody where you feel so close to them that they're kind of like you."

Some tracks on the album continued to carry the torch for punk rock with *Recoil* being the most 'punky'. The initial ideas for this song came from John McGeoch, but along with *Burst*, it was developed by the whole group in the lead up to recording. *Shot By Both Sides* was completely reworked as the band wanted to add keyboards to the track to reflect the way it was being played live now that Dave Formula was on board. The original master tape went missing at the crucial time (according to Mick Glossop it later turned up in the tape library at The Manor – nobody had looked particularly carefully) – so instead of just adding keyboards to the original track it was completely rerecorded.

The influence of Dave Formula in the band was most evident on tracks like *Definitive Gaze, The Great Beautician In The Sky* and *Parade*. Although the writing credit for *Definitive Gaze* was Howard and John, Dave was able to develop it, from its original skeletal form, with different keyboard parts. He says, "When I joined, Magazine was essentially a guitar band. Although Bob's contributions were very important to those songs they were quite spiky whereas I'm much more layered. When I got involved, there was a lot of freedom to develop the sound."

Originally, the opening salvo of *Definitive Gaze* was a guitar riff that was transposed on to the bass. Howard wrote the chorus on flange guitar, which he attempted to play, "somewhat bodgedly" on the first John Peel session before deciding to leave the guitar playing to John McGeoch. He says, "I much prefer the arrangement that later became the one that was worked in to the live act. It starts with free form. We used it to open the set a lot because it's quite a good one – the sound guy can get levels on the drums and the instruments come in one at a time and he can get all the sound sorted. Everybody in the guise of being avant-garde can test their equipment!"

The title of the song originated from a fictional play that Ben Mandelson created – he and Howard remained friends after they both left Bolton Institute of Technology. Referring to the ideas behind the lyrics, Howard explains, "It wasn't saying real life's an awful thing. It was trying to go for a philosophical acceptance of what it was – everything is where it ought to be."

Musically, *The Great Beautician In The Sky* betrays Howard's fascination with the Jacques Brel period of Bowie's career. He wrote the simple descending keyboard phrase that opens the song and features throughout the first half and introduced the 'waltzing' time signature. Dave came up with the organ sound that was used and says, "I'm not a purist but I'm a real Hammond Organ fan. I also grew up having a sneaking, almost secret, regard for some aspects of theatre organs – just the grandeur of them and the scale. For this track I tried to play the organ as if I couldn't really play it – it's a very different technique to playing the piano, which is percussive. I made it more bizarre – more cabaret."

Parade was written whilst Dave was still sharing a flat with Martin Hannett. He recalls, "He had a separate music room – just a pile of synthesisers and my stuff and his stuff. I was messing about and the main melody for the introduction just came into my head." Barry Adamson contributed some further ideas and between them they developed a very complete piece of music. Howard came up with the lyrics, reflecting the uncertainties and ambiguities that were part of the currency of his work, later confirming that the song had certain voyeuristic elements to it. Dave recalls, "We had conversations about his lyrics – 'Howard – come on – what's that mean?' Generally he would be quite ambiguous about it."

Recalling his part in the development of the song, Barry laughs, "I had a chord sequence on guitar. I remember playing it and John McGeoch quite rightly and very succinctly pointing out to me that it was the same melody as Frank Ifield's *I Remember You*. Every time it got to that we would sing: 'I remember you!' We used to joke with each other – what we used to try and do was subvert Howard's lyrics and make them funny."

But he also confides, "I'd write stuff all the time but I didn't have the confidence to put my ideas forward. I was eighteen and the idea that was rejected in the rehearsal room became a point of standing whereby I really took a step back – and [laughs] made my own album on the side! In fact – the main thing I remember about Ridge Farm was staying out there after everyone had finished and making cassettes of my own ideas on the keyboards and John's effects and stuff. I feel guilty saying this, but as much as I was excited by everything I was excited by being able to be around these things."

He continues, "I was the group stoner at the time – my main extra curricular interest was smoking as much dope as I could and having as much of a laugh as I could. But I also had my finger on the pulse and it didn't help in me being taken as seriously as I might have been. By the same token Howard knew I was there for the right reasons and although he was driving it I was a strong force in the group."

When Magazine released *Real Life* in June 1978, the reception was overwhelmingly positive. "No one that has the slightest interest in the present and future of rock 'n' roll should rest until they've heard *Real Life*," wrote Chris Brazier in *Melody Maker*. "I have no doubt of this album's absolutely awesome quality. Quite simply, *Real Life* is the best and most exciting album I've heard this year, representing as boldly imaginative and significant a step forward as Television's *Marquee Moon* was last year, or to hang on a more obvious reference hook, as Roxy Music's debut was back in 1972."

Phil McNeil in *NME* was equally impressed, writing, "The songs all seem to be arranged to the last quaver – and very expertly arranged they are too. Meshes of riffs replace one another in meticulous, kaleidoscopic order, using the classic guitar/bass/drums/keyboards line-up to its full. Every song is blindingly arranged – never sticking to one format, often changing the established riff structure at will so that – for instance – a song might fade out on a new refrain constructed of other elements of the song."

According to Mark Kidel in *The Observer*: "Devoto's introspective lyrics reflect a total and paranoid rejection of our brave new world, but he never rants about it explicitly. It is just an atmosphere suggested by the dark hopelessness of all his material. He does not deal in tender affection or sugar coated optimism, but sings instead – in near spoken style – about his haunted inner world. The melodies, in keeping with the obliqueness of the words, are bittersweet rather than obvious, but always constructed in such a way as to make them instantly memorable."

Whilst the music and the musicianship were widely praised, a discussion point for some writers was Howard's vocal performance. Phil McNeil observed, "It is the most distinctive element, but at the same time Devoto's vocals are the most restricted and – face it – just plain weak constituent here." Tim Lott in *Record Mirror* described his vocals as "heavily affected and slightly adenoidal," saying, "they wheeze, they crackle, they speed, crawl, warp and fade. Sometimes, like on *Recoil* they can be uncontrolled and irritating. Then, on *The Great Beautician In The Sky* they have a bite and punch-drunk slur that seep menace and sinew."

John Leckie argues that *Real Life* stands up well amongst today's music. He says, "For me it's one of the best records I've done. All the keyboard technology came from that period. There was so much being invented – every week there was a new gadget. Also, it's not recorded on computer but recorded on tape. There were no click tracks – nowadays most bands record with a click metronome – we never did that unless you wanted to use it as an effect. The album was recorded with the guitar, bass, drums and guide vocal all playing together. The band played live – this is why this record lasts. There's something in the space between the notes that allows your ear to live with repeated listenings. A lot of music today – it's in perfect tune, perfect time – on the first listen it sounds fantastic but you tire of it. It's like watching the same film over and over or hearing the same joke. Think of The Beatles' music – even now when you listen to it you always hear something you haven't heard before and you've been listening to it for thirty years."

He continues, "It's got something to do with the human tempo, the heart beat and also the resonance of it. Drum machines and guitar tuners were rare. Everything was tuned by ear to the piano or to each other – so it had its own kind of harmonious resonance that really isn't there now because everything's perfect and if it's not perfect it's corrected in the computer. Your ears are attuned to that – whereas in those days your ears were attuned to the whole thing rather than the details. This is one of those records I'm proud of because you can listen to it so many times."

Following the release of second single *Touch And Go* in April 1978, and before the release of *Real Life*, the band had undertaken a club and college tour travelling together in Andrew Graham-Stewart's Range Rover and taking in ten venues around England. Andrew remembers these early tours as being rather haphazard – but as having a tremendous amount of energy. He says, "Gigs at that level in those days were totally chaotic – particularly in terms of any band that had any punk connections. There was a hard core of people turning up at these gigs with the sole intent of causing havoc – getting up on stage, spitting at the artists. It always ended up on the road crew and they got pissed off. There was usually violence of some sort somewhere but those gigs had to be done. If you were going to progress there was no other way of doing it."

To promote *Real Life,* their biggest tour to date was arranged in the summer of 1978. Writing in *Sounds*, about the Bradford gig, Paul Chautauqua captured the sense of theatricality that pervaded Magazine's performances at that time: "Huge cheer as the lights dim. Air of intense anticipation. Shadows on stage. Lights flash up. Outlined across the stage, four of the band begin playing nightmare catcalls and whispers to each other, the music resounding in some strange oscillatory rhythm. Then Devoto appears, popping up beside Dave Formula's keyboards. Dressed in red shirt and with his gaunt face, the flaming image of Dracula's castle bursts open the music and we're off into the first number. Vampirically perched on his mike stand, Devoto lifts his voice gently, seductively..."

Prevented from closing the tour at the Drury Lane Theatre, because according to Moss Empires they 'verged on punk' and would 'lower the tone of the theatre', Magazine wrapped things up instead at the Lyceum on 30 July. Howard had read a reference to one of the Mekons looking like him so had invited him to appear on stage during the opening number. Howard describes the scene, "The band went on and started the number – he and I were in the wings. He went out on stage and took the microphone. I was singing live from the side but he'd tried to rehearse it a bit so he tried to lip synch with me. After the first verse I walked on and started playing the keyboard a bit along with Dave so there was two of us on stage for about five seconds and then he walked off the other side and I sang the second verse. He got all the applause when he

69

walked on."

Live, as well as in the studio, it was clear that many of the songs on *Real Life* leant themselves towards making full use of Dave Formula's prowess on keyboards and synthesisers – especially *Definitive Gaze*. Dave says, "As it developed and I integrated my keyboards more into the band, you could see the identity was developing." Speaking retrospectively, John McGeoch said, "We certainly welcomed Dave bringing in stuff like that because it gave us much more of a vocabulary. There wasn't a master plan, but we were reacting against head banging because everybody was doing it. The Buzzcocks and the Pistols and a few other bands were the original ones to play like that, and then suddenly every town had about twenty bands all sounding exactly the same. While we were involved in the energy side of things, we didn't just want to sound like The Clash."

However, not all members of the group were comfortable with the way the sound was developing and Martin Jackson in particular began to show his discomfort. Howard recalls, "He developed a slightly strange personality – the sort of thing that made you think 'this person's not very happy with how things are going and therefore perhaps that explains the slightly strange behaviour'. I'm sure we'd have been going, 'What's up with Martin?'"

Barry says, "He was quite pissed off with the direction the group had been taking. Especially since Dave Formula had brought this new sound and colour to the thing. It obviously gave way to do things like *Parade*. He was so pissed off that one day he refused to play it. I said to him, 'Why won't you play *Parade*?' and he said, 'It's like bloody tea room music'."

Although slightly offended by his remarks, Barry understood Martin's concerns. He says, "He was a punk purist and I think for him, *Parade* being on the first album was an indication of where things were going to go. I had a foot in both camps. I was slightly wary that all these keyboards were arriving. I felt that the original electric piano had a spooky quality, which I felt laid out the musical landscape beautifully in terms of Magazine's sound. On the other hand I thought it was a chance to expand and make another sound that was unheard of."

Of Martin, Dave says, "I wasn't convinced with his playing – never was. I thought he was the weak link musically. I told Howard on the train on the way back from mixing *Real Life* that I didn't think Martin was up to it. We'd very quickly got sophisticated while we were making the album. Martin still had a punk attitude to everything and that kind of didn't fit in a way. Barry, John and Howard were and are very bright people all thinking and operating in one way and Martin didn't fit mentally or musically."

He admits that there was a fall-out between himself and Martin whilst they were working on *Parade*. He says, "I'd always had this idea in my head of using a drum machine. Martin didn't like the fact that we were using synthesisers and certainly didn't like the fact that we were using a drum machine even though he was still playing on it. I remember him saying to me when we were sat in the control room, 'You and your fucking drum machines and synthesisers – you'll be the death of this band'."

For Andrew Graham-Stewart, Martin came across as "astonishingly immature". He says, "He was very young and got very easily upset about things." Martin says now that his frustration stemmed from what he saw as the lack of momentum on the band's part. He says, "I felt – this stuff is just going to disappear – and that's what happened. I mean I never thought we were going to be huge but when you saw that people in the audience knew every song and every track – to me that was just allowed to go. There was a momentum building up which was lost. John Peel played the whole of the album on his show but we weren't doing anything to promote it. We weren't anywhere to be seen and it was kind of a waste of time and I just lost interest. I wasn't sure enough of myself to say that I had doubts."

He continues, "Also – I'd got a bit frustrated with playing the drums. It wasn't an instrument I chose, I just fell into it by accident. I was beginning to get a bit fed up with it – I was more interested in music than drums. I actually only carried on playing drums for a few years after and then got into writing. I did also worry that it was going a bit 'prog'... I think if we'd been a bit busier I'd have been a lot happier. There seemed to be huge gaps where we were doing nothing at all." He continues, "I said I was going to leave when we were rehearsing for the tour because nothing happened, not much was going on. I trundled down to the rehearsal rooms and had a chat about it. Howard was annoyed but there was no communication. Frustrations had got the better of me. I regret the way it happened but I would have continued to have misgivings."

The band advertised for a new drummer and embarked on auditions where according to Barry, "drummer after drummer after drummer came along". Paul Spencer, who describes himself as a "bit of a seventies rocker", came to the auditions via an advert in *Melody Maker*. Having no idea who the 'name band with a record deal' were that were 'looking for a drummer', he had phoned the Manchester number to be informed that the band were in fact Magazine. None the wiser, he bought *Real Life* and practised solidly and was excited to be asked to join them in time for their autumn European tour supporting Patti Smith.

Although Paul had been unaware of Magazine prior to joining them, he soon appreciated what they were doing and at the warm-up gig at Eric's in Liverpool he got a sense of the excitement surrounding the band. He says, "I could tell they were a cut above a lot of the bands that were around at the time. Musically, Dave Formula really raised the bar." He also reveals, "I knew they needed someone capable of fulfilling their touring commitments but I did join them thinking I was becoming part of the band."

The Patti Smith tour was Magazine's first and only time as a support band. Taking in West Germany along with a few other European cities it was an eye-opener for the still teenage Barry who says, "I had a very strong sense of seeing the world for the first time. Just seeing the contrast between east and west – it was like a party going on when you came back to the west." Howard also gained a lot from the experience and remembers, "It was the first time I'd been in a place where I felt 'these people don't want us here'. It was quite striking. I'd never been to Germany before and of course you had to drive the corridor through part of East Germany to get to West Berlin – a little bit of *Feed The Enemy* came from that."

Andrew Graham-Stewart recalls the tour as being "hard work", largely because Magazine were quite unknown in Europe and the audiences in the vast sports halls were indifferent. Dave recalls, "It was a bad experience and I was getting more and more pissed off with it. We'd go on and it was like we weren't there. It was pretty much a disaster really apart from the last date in Brussels, which was a big venue, but not a sports hall, so we had some control over the sound. We'd sold records and were recognised and seen as an interesting band whereas hardly anyone had heard of us in Germany. We went down really well in Brussels and almost stole the show. It was a good one to end on."

Howard also found it difficult adjusting to the position of being the lesser lights. He says, "Even if only fifty people turn up and you're the main attraction that tends to feel better than fifty people who like you a lot embedded in two thousand. I think I cocked a bit of an attitude with the audience and they didn't like me. I remember being bombarded with Styrofoam cups in Munich."

The band remember Patti Smith as being an uncooperative touring partner whose main connection with them was her interest in one member of their touring crew. Howard says, "I do distinctly recall the general vibe we got from Patti Smith was not, 'Hello, welcome to my tour fellow new wave musicians' – more that she completely blanked us and almost made a point of making a play for our roadie." Paul laughs, "We kind of suspected it was going on – he always used to wear this red and black checked shirt. We knew for sure it was all true when she played the whole of her set wearing his 'lumberjack shirt'." In fact, Barry says, "I remember being shocked at some of the states she was in – but one of my main memories is that I was the go-between between her and our roadie – for being the go-between she gave me a plectrum that said 'rock 'n' roll nigger' on it."

Paul remembers, "She was a complete nutcase – she would often finish the show by climbing on top of the PA speakers, playing her clarinet and people wouldn't know if it was part of the show or not. She was also quite unfriendly and very mean spirited. There was no camaraderie. She had a girlfriend and they travelled in one Mercedes whilst the rest of her band travelled in an-

Captured by John Leckie's camera – most probably at the Greyhound, Croyden,
30 April 1978

Promotional photographs, 1979
Above: John Doyle, Howard Devoto, Barry Adamson, Dave Formula, John McGeoch

Secondhand Daylight Tour 1979.
Photos by John Leckie (probably Top Rank, Sheffield, 18 April 1979) and unknown.

Howard saw this image of *The Geek* by Ian Pollock (see page 161) and subsequently used the original illustration on the front of *Secondhand Daylight* (page 206), 1979

Lyric for *Permafrost* (page 180), showing the way John had set his flanger in rehearsals Taken from Howard's notebook

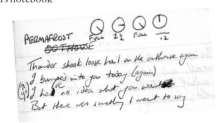

Photography by Richard Rayner-Canham using a special hand-built camera (see page 162) featured on the inner gatefold sleeve for *Secondhand Daylight* (below) and subsequent promotional material (above), 1979

On tour with Magazine, from John Doyle's camera, 1979 and 1980

other." Dave recalls, "She was particularly indulgent with sound checks. We'd have a sound check scheduled and we'd all arrive on time and be sat in the hall and she'd go half an hour past our deadline, then an hour past our deadline and if we got five minutes we were doing well. Effectively every other gig she'd balls the sound check up for us. She did think she could play this clarinet and we'd spend half an hour listening to her play absolute bollocks down the PA – which she'd use maybe for two minutes in one of her songs."

As was Howard's wont, he kept himself pretty much to himself on the tour. He says, "I didn't have much to do with Patti Smith's entourage. I'm not much of a mixer on the road – it takes my all to maintain the appearance of psychic intactness so I often don't mix very much on the road with other people." Andrew Graham-Stewart recalls, "The rest of the band were always indulging in typical rock 'n' roll on tour antics – after a gig they would drink as much as possible and see where that led. Howard didn't – he just didn't enjoy that sort of thing. He didn't indulge in excess."

Paul Spencer felt that he and Howard "connected" and in fact they travelled together on the tour. As a fan of American rock music himself, Paul was surprised and amused to discover that Howard greatly enjoyed Bruce Springsteen's *Darkness On The Edge Of Town* and it was a fixture on the car's audio system at the time. Although he had some rapport with Dave, Paul felt that he never really got on with John or Barry. He says, "John and Barry shared a lot of private jokes and it all felt a bit cliquey. John was very confident whereas Barry seemed a little insecure – almost under John's spell. We never made that extra connection that would have kept us together."

Despite the negatives, the band and management recognised that the tour was a step up and they got a glimpse of what touring on the next level would be like. Andrew confirms that some of the band learned a great deal from the experience and in some ways it made them doubly determined to reach new audiences. There were also highlights for the band along the way – as when Iggy Pop put in an appearance at the Berlin gig. Paul says, "That was the most exciting night. It was about the coolest thing that could have happened to us. He came backstage and then took us to a trendy club – I remember it was horribly lit with neon light. There was a band playing and we ended up getting up on stage and playing a couple of Magazine songs." Howard remembers his thoughts at the time: "Ah I'm starting to meet people now, a different part of the world. What an international life I'm starting to have."

Whilst on tour in Europe, the band were showcased on French TV when they performed in a Paris theatre with French jazz rock outfit Magma. On returning to the UK they were scheduled to put in an appearance on *The Old Grey Whistle Test* – the most serious minded rock programme on British television at the time. Mindful of their British audience and image, the band decided to address the issue of Paul's hair. He says, "All through the tour I had quite long hair which wasn't a problem. I hadn't got the same sort of thrift store look they had but none of that mattered all the way through the tour until we got to Brussels. Barry and John took me to a chic hairdressers and made me get my hair cut really short. Of course this was in preparation for *The Old Grey Whistle Test*. I needed to look a bit more like I belonged in the band!"

A previous edition of *The Old Grey Whistle Test* had aired one of the band's three promotional videos: *The Light Pours Out Of Me, Motorcade* and *Touch And Go*. These were filmed onstage at the Rainbow and Howard recalls, "That was another time I was incredibly pissed off – with the guy who was filming it – and probably that came over in my (mimed) performance. I can't remember why – he was probably just a 'churn it through the sausage machine' type of guy and I probably wanted a little more attention. I can't recall him having any real ideas."

For their first live appearance on the programme, the band showcased *Definitive Gaze* and upcoming single *Give Me Everything*. Howard found the experience marginally better than *Top of the Pops* primarily because it wasn't mimed. It was to be Paul's swansong with the band however as shortly afterwards he received a phone-call from Andrew informing him that the band didn't really feel things were working out – and that was the last he heard from them.

John Doyle was recruited as drummer after John McGeoch spotted him playing with his band Idiot Rouge at the Fresher's Ball at Manchester Polytechnic in October 1978. John says, "We'd just finished the gig and I was walking to the dressing room when John asked me almost sheepishly if I was interested in auditioning. I rang in sick to work and did an audition on the Monday. On Wednesday I phoned in and resigned from work – on Friday I was in Munich doing a TV show." Howard remembers, "He came along to the rehearsal studios and we tried him out. Again – nobody's straight in of course. It's then you do a trial – if you're going to coop yourselves up in cars, vans, dressing rooms and pub crawls you need to be able to get on with them on a few levels as well as being able to do the job."

John recalls, "I didn't consider it to be a big break – I just considered it to be the next band. There was no way I wasn't going to go for it – I had no responsibilities. I was just twiddling my thumbs. I had no idea of the scale of it at the time. I was aware of Magazine but I hadn't really heard them. That side of music hadn't hit where I was coming from. I wasn't involved in the more image conscious fashion life style side of things – of being in the hip clubs. That was kind of hidden to me so I had to immerse myself in what they were doing. I couldn't go along and be anything other than myself and fortunately musically it worked."

"I think I brought something that they hadn't had before which was a more funk attitude rather than a rock attitude. They – and especially Barry – took to that immediately. The song they were working on at the time was *Give Me Everything*. They played me the riff and I played naturally what I would do which was, I think, quite twisted from how they'd been rehearsing it. I wouldn't say I fitted in head wise – I didn't dress fashionably. They knew what looked good and what was in vogue. I didn't kick up a fuss or make a noise that would make me an irritant and I just fitted in. As I became more aware of what it was all about I still just went along with it – I didn't question it."

With John on board, the band recorded a performance for BBC Radio's *In Concert* programme and embarked on a tour of UK venues, commencing at Portsmouth. Along the way they again fell victim to the residue of punk as Middlesbrough Town Hall officials cancelled their date in the wake of The Clash's lively appearance at the venue. Dogged by, in some cases, an unpredictable mix and wretched acoustics, reviewers were however generally held in thrall by the live Magazine experience. Paul du Noyer reviewed the London Venue gigs and wrote, "The group's true worth lies in their awesome abilities as a musical unit. Their sound is cold and strong and seems to bristle with ominous potential. Devoto's dry and bitter vocals curl and climb about the music.... the classically sculptured features animated by the ghost of a mocking smile."

Present at the same gigs, John Orme wrote, "One of the initially attractive and continuingly compulsive qualities of Magazine is the band's ability to create wide-screen musical pictures while maintaining the drive and urgency that marks it as one of today's creations. There were times in the set when McGeoch and bass player Barry Adamson worked together with total and seductive efficiency. *Motorcade* took them from the jaunty, slightly menacing opening atmosphere, through a persuasive build-up to a slipstream beat with Devoto's harsh vocals straining against the metal of the guitar as Formula coaxed the band along with spiral keyboard motifs: a thrilling and powerful performance."

However, both du Noyer and Orme held reservations about Howard's ability to cut it live. Orme wrote, "The spirit of Devoto the writer and musician hangs dominant over the proceedings, but Devoto the singer and frontman goes about his business with a lack of passion, clarity and persuasion. The now infamous house PA left full appreciation of his lyrics to lip-readers, and certainly during the opening number Devoto had the bored charisma of a passenger waiting for a train as Magazine worked their distinctive magic behind."

Moreover, the backlash against Howard in particular seemed to be gathering pace with journalists seemingly resentful of what some perceived to be Howard's air of intellectual superiority. In an earlier otherwise favourable piece about the band, Phil McNeill still managed to have a dig at the frontman by writing in *NME,* "I saw Devoto in the flesh not long ago – tripping over his mike stand at the Roundhouse and inadvertently puncturing his obnoxious display of self-important co-o-ol. I also saw him just last week – making a complete prat of himself on *The Old Grey Whistle Test* – where his personal performance was probably the most pretentious that show has ever played host to."

Earlier in the year, journalist Jon Savage had shown an understanding of the processes at work here as he observed of Magazine, "They've been subjected to a disproportionate amount of press, concentrating overly, in the lack of much

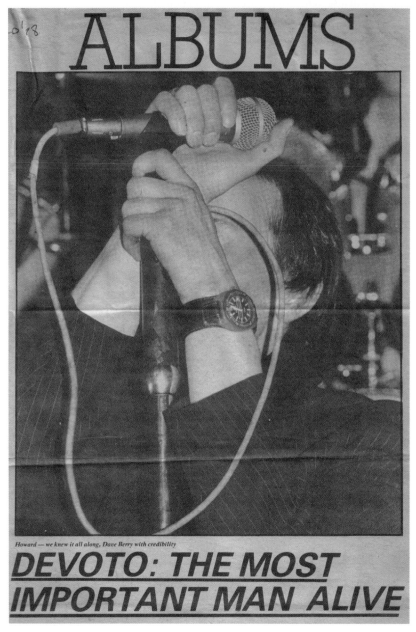

ALBUMS

Howard — we knew it all along, Dave Berry with credibility

DEVOTO: THE MOST IMPORTANT MAN ALIVE

NME, 3 June 1978

else, on Howard Devoto's 'enigma'." Jon watched with, "amusement and then irritation" as he said, "Writers jumped in with both left feet to proclaim a front page saviour, thereby raising expectations that no one could have fulfilled. When Magazine naturally failed to, still working to reach their tenth gig, a backlash started with fuel added by others who took exception to Devoto's refusal to dictate and package the answer to all our problems in marketable slogans through corporate channels."

But it was the release of *Give Me Everything* in November 1978 that saw new depths plumbed in the relationship between Howard and the press. Ironically – because in keeping with Howard's dislike of doing things in the accepted record business way, *Give Me Everything* was released with no marketing campaign whatsoever. No review copies were sent out; the official Virgin line being, "People who want the record will find out about it and buy it anyway."

Maybe this (non) strategy irked *Sounds* reviewer Dave McCullough for he mounted an almost personal attack on the band and Howard in particular. He wrote: "At last I have Howie and chums sussed. They're really The Muppets in disguise laughing their scraggy-heads off while the hundred thousand punks STILL take them seriously. This is dreadful – the lyrics proving more cringe-worthy even than usual. 'You're so oblique and easy'. Look – Howie – you're as much a poet as Len Fairclough is a poet – so why don'tcha sod off – you baldy little pain?"

Howard's response was to send Dave McCullough a cheque for ten pounds with the words, "Your review of *Give Me Everything* was so unbelievably sympathetic, was so to the point that this £10 of my enthusiastic and shrieking money must go to you. You're not so oblique but you're so easy. You must have it. I hope that you see that. I'm sorry it couldn't be more. Please cash it. Have a Christmas, Howard."

Howard recalls now, "I remember the consultation with Al Clarke, the Virgin press officer, and he said, 'You know they'll print it don't you?' And they did. Again – it was me trying to not be bland – to do something a bit different. Insult me and I'll give you some money – feed the enemy. It still does amaze me how people can write things that would just earn them a punch basically if it was done in 'real life'."

Despite sniping by some corners of the press the band finished 1978 on a musical and creative high. Speaking in late 1978, Dave said, "The dream is happening now. The great thing is writing a song and honing it – knowing that we don't need too many explanations within the band to get exactly what we want out of our music." With the ultimate Magazine line-up of Devoto, Adamson, McGeoch, Formula and Doyle in place the band looked ready to go from strength to strength.

PAYOLA BY POST

Dave McCullough
Sounds
40 Long Acre
London WC2E 9JT

Dear Payee,

Your review of Give Me Everything was so
unbelievably sympathetic, was so to the
point that this £10 of my enthusiastic
and shrieking money must go to you.

You're not so oblique but you're so easy.

You must have it.
I hope you see that.
I'm sorry it couldn't be more.
Please cash it.

Have a Christmas,

Howard.

Howard Devoto.

15th December 1978

Lloyds Bank Limited

19-10   MANCHESTER BRANCH   30-95-42
         53 KING STREET MANCHESTER M60 2ES

PAY *David McCullough* ————————————— OR ORDER

Ten Pounds   £10-00

                                          DEVOTO

                                          H Devoto.

199729 30 95 42 0735921

Chapter Five —

I was cold
at an equally
cold place …

Secondhand Daylight

THE FIRST FEW wintry months of 1979 saw Magazine back in the studio recording their follow-up album *Secondhand Daylight*. The confidence that had been engendered with the critical and commercial success of *Real Life* showed itself in the band's ambition approaching this album and they were ready to push the musical boundaries even further. *Parade* – the closing track on the debut album – had already hinted at a possible direction. "We were moving even further away from punk and into the idea of soundscapes," remembered Barry some time later, "music that was both emotional and descriptive."

Accordingly, soundtrack supremo John Barry was Magazine's first choice to produce the album. Indulgent of the band's wishes, Simon Draper and Virgin approached Barry, who was at the time a tax exile living in Los Angeles. Although Barry was apparently agreeable, the financial implications of the band relocating to LA to record proved insurmountable. Second choice Tony Visconti (who had worked on *Low* with David Bowie) was either unavailable or too expensive. The band turned instead to a young engineer called Colin Thurston, who'd worked with Visconti on Bowie's *Heroes* and on *Lust For Life* by Iggy Pop.

Secondhand Daylight was recorded at Good Earth Studios, Soho, London and on the Manor Mobile. Howard remembers, "Colin was the compromise but he knew that we were up for a bit more of a radical sound and so he picked that baton up and tried to go with it. The difference in the overall sound of *Real Life* and *Secondhand Daylight* is very marked I would say – and that's Colin. John still had the same guitar set up – MXR flanger [mounted on the mic stand], compressor and modified Marshall amp. Barry was probably flanging his bass a lot more then too but the big overall sound was what the producer was all about."

The new sound wasn't one that was imposed on the band by the producer however. As John McGeoch explained later, "We didn't actually want to have heavy sounding guitars all the way through. It was partly due to me that the guitar was down. We really did stretch the studio, we did use lots of effects." Howard elucidated at the time, "My role was essentially an arranger, a diplomat, having to balance the egos of everybody else – though being the lyric writer gives you a lot of power over the ultimate form of the song. Dave Formula was a lot more confident on this album – and while McGeoch could be quite spiky, he was also less persistent, so he got a bit squeezed out." Dave remembers, "I wrote the music for *Back To Nature, Feed The Enemy* – both very dark synth sounds – and *I Wanted Your Heart.*" Describing *Feed The Enemy* he says, "I don't know why I sat down and came up with that intro – I wasn't aiming to do anything particularly epic, I was just trying to see how far I could push the synthesiser. It was still quite early days for synths."

Colin Thurston reveals in a 1995 interview with Dave Simpson that John McGeoch didn't actually have a lot to play on the album – mainly rhythm parts. He also recalls John's frustration whilst trying to get a good sound from one of the first synth guitars that the band had rented. He says, "We had closed circuit TV looking into the studio, and all I saw was him taking it off and throwing it across the room. It hit something and the neck snapped. We went back to the hire company and told them that it fell off a chair. The guys said 'Do you realise that this thing has got a metal pole down the centre?! There's no way it could have broken falling off a chair.'"

Of course John McGeoch still made his presence felt on the album, most notably with the solo on *Permafrost*. To many people's surprise, however, the track over which he actually had the most influence was *The Thin Air* – the instrumental that opens side two on the vinyl album. Howard says, "That was John's piece, which is kind of curious because I'm not sure there's very much guitar on it. But he'd written it all on keyboards and when he played it to us I listened to it and went 'Hmmm – nuances of Pink Floyd in there, John.' I couldn't tune into it lyrically so the idea evolved to try it as an instrumental."

John explained the genesis of the track in 1980. He said, "It's just that in Manchester we had a rehearsal studio all to ourselves in a guy's cellar. We used to leave all our equipment set up so any time anyone wanted to go in they'd just go down there. One day Barry was with me and we went down there and recorded it. I wrote it on a guitar, and all Dave's keyboards were there, we just messed around and layered it up a bit."

Recording this album was John Doyle's first real studio experience. He says, "I was just along for the ride trying to make out that I knew what I was doing. At the time the drums had to be recorded first – drum machines were not so common – so my performance was critical. Fortunately I didn't realise that at the time. We did rehearse the songs – not to death but certainly within an inch of their lives. In essence there was a live performance in each of the recordings." Working in the days before click tracks and sophisticated editing tools, this was especially the case with the drums as there wasn't the opportunity to repair them.

Again, in 1995, Colin Thurston reflected on his work with Magazine and the recording of *Secondhand Daylight*. He describes the band – and Howard in particular – as being way ahead of their time. Of Howard he says, "He was a very quiet guy – very intense. If you made a comment about something and he wasn't sure what you'd said, he'd grill you for ten minutes to get out exactly what you were trying to say. There were no flippant remarks around Howard because he'd look at you and his eyes would sort of widen and he'd just turn away and you'd think, 'What the hell is he thinking now?'"

He continues, "He was very into himself. If I would ask for some written lyrics to accompany a vocal he would say, 'Well. I've got some little bits of scrap paper. You can write them down but I'll probably change them in the next take.' He was a hard worker in the studio. If a vocal wasn't quite the way I liked it or he liked it, he'd stand there for an hour, two hours, and do that vocal. But, invariably, it would be, 'I don't want to get too clinical. I want to keep it semi-rough. So, if we get it right first time I'd like to hold onto it'."

The experiences of the band whilst touring West Germany the previous year informed some of the writing for this album. There was more of a collective shared understanding reflected in the lyrics, based in part on the landscapes they'd been travelling through. Album opener *Feed The Enemy* combined these experiences together with references from Howard's reading material. He says, "I'd read about the shutting down of all the TV and radio stations in Czechoslovakia in 1968 until there's one left ... and then there's a story I'd read in America about a plane crash and everyone came out to have a look at it."

The track set the tone for the whole album, which for one reviewer was like "being ushered into a new era and a strange, bleak, alien landscape." Howard remembers that the choice of this track to open the album was the one of the few times that Simon Draper voiced a strong opinion about the band's material. He says, "We would generally find with Virgin an infuriating lack of feedback from them about what might be a single and so forth. But this time Simon was like, 'Does it have to start with *Feed The Enemy*? Like a downbeat thing?' I definitely felt – yes – it does! It's serious."

He elaborates, "For the first three albums I always knew the sequence of the songs – my sense of performance I suppose. An album is a performance lasting about three quarters of an hour and therefore what should be the ebb and flow of that three quarters of an hour? I would know what should be at the beginning and end of a side without even the lengthy business of sequencing it. That would have taken the assistant engineer an hour, hour and a half to cut all the tape around so that you could then listen to it. I would just know in my head."

Howard refutes the claim from some quarters that there are no upbeat or danceable tracks on the album. He cites *Talk To The Body, Believe That I Understand* and *Rhythm Of Cruelty* as being up-tempo, with the latter released as a single in March 1979 and boasting "one of John's most exuberant guitar riffs". Dave adds, "In *I Wanted Your Heart* there's a whole section that's just improvised where it all goes a bit crazy with piano and bass. That's a real contrast rhythmically and harmonically to *Feed The Enemy* and *Back To Nature* – almost jaunty in its feel, but not in the lyrics which are consistent with the rest."

Howard concedes that *Secondhand Daylight* is more uncompromising than *Real Life* and describes it as "a process of going inside oneself." He continues, "An awful lot of it's about how certain everyone seems to me and I don't feel certain at all about hardly anything. All that opening of *Cut Out Shapes* is ironic – in other words, 'I'm not confident at all'." Howard was also continuing the theme from the first album of playing with his own feelings of power. He says, "My friend Richard Boon at one point suggested a title for the album – *Tales of Power* – which is the title of the fourth Carlos Castaneda book." However he reflects, "It would have been hard to have named the album that because of the hippy connotations. But because it was a bit wicked and because it wasn't a bad description of contents I quite liked it as a title. I remember mentioning it and Mr McGeoch going, 'Oh – no!' I didn't feel strongly enough about it to fight it."

He elaborates, "As soon as you start talking about relationships you start talking about power anyway. *Back To Nature* stated it most baldly – 'I want to walk where the power is.' Virtually every line has a double meaning." The title came from Howard's experiences on a trip to the wilds of Scotland with manager Andrew Graham-Stewart. He says, "I couldn't relax there and I was getting nothing out of it. I wasn't in the right frame of mind to be away from cultural civilisation. I was so engrossed in my 'career' that I wasn't able to just unwind and enjoy the scenery. There wasn't even any electricity where we were staying! I thought: 'Back to nature? It's not doing anything for me'."

Whilst Howard was wrestling with abstract thoughts around the theme of power, Barry was becoming aware of shifting sands within the group. He observes in hindsight, "I felt a kind of power thing going on – there's the leader of the group and everyone's coming after you to get their piece of power. But I think that makes for great dynamics – that makes for good music." Speaking of Howard, he continues, "I did also notice him toying with certain lyrical ideas and setting up something which perhaps aided the mystery of where they had come from. I felt slightly ill at ease wondering 'what's going on here?'"

Barry suggests that part of the strength of the lyrics is that you can attach your own scenario. For his part, Howard allows that his lyrics are open to interpretation, but that "if you get it too wrong, I'll have to tell you. Some songs can be subject to interpretations you don't like." Speaking of the song *Permafrost*, he says, "The song started with the line 'I will drug you and fuck you' and evolved from there. I've defended it against being a rape fantasy. It's supposed to be tender really. Trying to find a little pleasure, a little something, in a very difficult world."

He continues, "I know I'm being very difficult and I understand why people go on about its icy atmosphere – after all it is called *Permafrost*! Dave *did* do those icicle keyboards. I remember being thrilled when I picked up on him starting to do that when we were rehearsing and writing it. John McGeoch also contributed heavily to the final sound of the track by virtue of the way he set his flanger in rehearsals." In fact, Howard made a note of these settings in his notebook so that the sound could be recaptured exactly when the song (which had the working title of *Outhouse*) was recorded in the studio.

Howard wasn't around when the track was mixed. He relates, "I remember going back to Good Earth and walking through the door to be met with 'We've mixed *Permafrost* do you want to hear it?' 'Oh – that's a bit presumptuous isn't it?! Anyway, go on then.' I remember Colin playing the tape and he'd done this thing with the effects on the vocal in the verses and then it goes completely dry in the choruses and so it becomes very close and it was fantastic! There was just one thing I didn't like. On the last chorus he'd put a great big emphatic repeat delay on the word 'fuck' and I just said 'that's got to go. But apart from that it's fine – well done!'"

The title *Permafrost* actually came from Howard reading a book about Russia. He also reveals, "'Sugar's sweet some of the time' was a line from about eight years earlier recapturing one of the first times I smoked dope – I remember I could switch off my sense of taste – it made biscuits taste like gravel." As observed by Nick Kent in *NME*, the track owes passing nods to both Iggy Pop and John Barry and is an appropriately chilling and seductive end to the album.

Most reviewers picked up on the 'wintry' feel to the album and in fact the winter it was recorded was one of the coldest in living memory. Howard dismisses the notion that this may have had some bearing on the feel of the album with the words, "Fanciful piffle!" Nevertheless, band members and producer alike have vivid memories of the freezing cold weather. John Doyle recalls, "I remember coming down from Manchester on the train with John to start recording. It was a real old train with no heating and blizzard conditions. We were absolutely freezing to death by the time we got off the train seven hours later. The image in my head was of *Brief Encounter* – it wasn't a steam train but it may as well have been."

Even Colin's first meeting with the band in Manchester was under similar circumstances. Speaking in 1995, he remembers, "I drove up there in a blizzard – snow flying everywhere – saw them go through about ten or twelve songs in a little basement place that they rehearsed in and came back to London. I think they were a bit nervous and so I didn't tell them it was my first production."

The album was completed in the Manor Mobile at a place called The Farmyard, which at the time was just a rehearsal set-up. Colin recalled the atmosphere at the time in the same article, "It was all rather strange. Howard had to sit in one of the rooms to do a vocal and he was absolutely frozen. He was dressed up like a mad abominable snowman and I remember seeing the breath just falling off his face."

John Doyle has another memory of the Manor Mobile with its picturesque but snowy backdrop. He says, "I remember Barry and myself sat in the control room – we'd just come in out of a very bleak night, very cold and sobering. Then to be instantly blown away listening to John record the solo for *Permafrost* was utterly mesmerising – all we could do was gawp. The engineer, tape op and producer were all concentrating and as a result maybe missing the enormity of it. It was possibly one take; I may be wrong about that but it was so unusual, so ethereal. There was utter silence after it, everyone was speechless."

Barry has an equally vivid memory of mixing *Feed The Enemy* at Good Earth. Speaking to Mojo in 2000 he said, "I remember listening to the final mix at dawn and when the girl backing singers came in halfway through – I felt this sort of shiver all over – and thought – 'This is just fucking genius!' I thought it was going to be the record that would take us all the way – it was so cocky and bolshie and grand in its delivery. We saw ourselves as the host bastion of cold front reportage. We were very self-important."

The confidence the band felt on completion of the album however was severely dented when the reception the album received matched the climate in which it was recorded. The fact that it came in a gatefold sleeve, featured an instrumental track and keyboard heavy production, was too much for some reviewers to take and critic after critic fell back on easy jibes of a return to progressive (retrogressive?) rock.

Garry Bushell in *Sounds* was vitriolic, dispensing a torrent of scathing comments aimed at Magazine and Howard Devoto in particular. "What a nice glossy magazine and what a nice glossy gatefold cover. So nice. So arty – just like the old days," he sniped. Quoting *Feed The Enemy* he opined, "It would seem that the current yardstick of intellectualism is inability to communicate a single idea or emotion which is why Devoto – who consistently fails to communicate anything save his own undoubted superiority over the rest of the human race – is held so highly by that section of the music press that equates pretension with Art. If the border exists it is between Devoto and Real life – and the music press's self-conscious Intellectuals are his border guards."

He continued, "Come on – let's walk down Memory Lane the Magazine way. Let's regurgitate fifth-rate *Low* period pieces. Let's plonk plonk plonk with ponderous sub-Pink Floydery. Let's do the Wallpaper Waltz. This is not pushing back the barriers – it's frighteningly bland Conservatism – and what is really annoying is knowing it will be hailed in certain quarters as something Brave and New. Don't be fooled." His final flourish was to ask, "How long will it be before Magazine need a juggernaut for their synthesisers?"

Nick Kent in *NME* was independently minded enough to buck the trend and discussed the album in terms of its own merits stating, "Where previously there was half-realised potential, there is now an austere sense of authority to the music... Magazine have well and truly become a group." He also declared, "*Back To Nature* is the finest song and performance Devoto and Magazine have ever executed. Devoto finally finds his voice – a terse, uncompromising instrument – and lets fly with floods of imagery that owe nothing to anyone – while Magazine match him punch for punch."

However, the best James Truman in *Melody Maker* could manage was the verdict, "two steps forward, two steps back", whilst branding the group in danger of becoming "self-conscious art-rock/future-shock poseurs". He condemned the album to be played "incessantly in university halls – public-school studies – and the bedrooms of tortured adolescents (male – of course)," summing it up with, "Curiously asexual and soulless – it invites analysis rather than reaction: an unsociable record."

The band were surprised and hurt by the press reaction. Looking back, Barry says, "It *was* disappointing when the reviews came out. We had an expectation that things would go from strength to strength and become absolutely huge." Musing on later events, he says, "I think if we'd stayed together, ultimately we'd have had a chance." Howard reveals, "Disappointment is putting it mildly! If you think something you've done is great you generally think most people will also think it's great." According to Barry, Howard was to later tell him that he had been devastated by the critical response.

At the time, wounded and on the defensive, the band took refuge in blaming the production. After all, it was a recurring theme in reviews at the time. James Truman again: "Colin Thurston weighs in with a full wide screen sound which – while reflecting some of the band's more ponderous arrangements – often seems overbearing and needlessly extravagant – effectively burying the songs in layer upon layer of icily dramatic textures." However, Howard now realises that the criticism was unfair and reflecting on the album says, "I think it had a handful of really good tracks and some quite quickly written things that could have been a bit better honed. I think Colin Thurston's production was very good."

For Howard then, looking back, it was perhaps a case of hubris – pride comes before a fall. Barry, for his part, regards *Secondhand Daylight* as his personal favourite Magazine album. He says, "To me, some of the sounds on there were actually dispelling this idea of 'prog rock'. Here was this great chord sequence for the opening of *Feed The Enemy*, which rhythmically was leaning more towards where I was coming from. There was a little 'progrockiness' but to me it was existential in the way it was coming together."

He continues, "For me *Secondhand Daylight* is the quintessential Magazine album. Howard was really on top of his game, coming up with all these ideas for the artwork. Any doubts I had re synthesisers were dispelled on that record and all the themes resonate perfectly for me. On a personal level I was up to speed with the intensity, coming into my own and seeing some success – championing the fact that we were a force to be reckoned with. I was a bit baffled actually by the critical response to *Secondhand Daylight*. I thought,

'They're idiots, they don't get it.'"

In retrospect, Howard feels that some of the criticism could have been deflected at the time by addressing two of the things that made reviewers suspicious. He says, "I do think the instrumental *The Thin Air* really affected how people heard that album. There *are* nuances of Pink Floyd in there. I think that and the gatefold sleeve led to the 'prog rock's back' slant to the criticism. If I thought changing the sleeve was going to offset thirty per cent of the criticism then I would change the sleeve." Almost as an afterthought he adds, "I was probably getting up people's noses at that point as well."

In fact, apart from the record reviews, press coverage of Magazine had subsided in the early part of 1979 – although Howard prompted one more bizarre encounter with *Sounds* journalist Dave McCullough. Picking up the threads of their 1978 spat around the release of *Give Me Everything*, McCullough was invited to meet Howard for a chat in what he describes as "the environs of a deserted, derelict building in Chelsea" – in reality Summa Studios, Magazine's rehearsal space. By Howard's admission, he was trying to do something a little different, even to 'freak' the journalist out a little. Inevitably though, McCullough had the last word as he penned the article for *Sounds*.

He described the scene: "I enter a smooth, long warehouse which is pitch dark save the top right-hand corner where three white boards make a sort of rectangle in the centre of which is the only light, a piercing, slanted beacon. I stand in the middle of the area, bemused more than scared or nervous. The whole thing seems so crass and hatched. Like Magazine themselves. All schemes and no real living ideas. And Howie appears from behind one of the boards, looking vaguely debonair and silly. He doesn't speak, merely puts his fingers to his lips in a gesture of silence and switches on what he later informs me is a tape of, wait for it, Balinese children singing, a horrible series of Hari-Krishna like squealing."

Although to Howard it was all to some extent a game, it was clear that the nature of his relationship with some parts of the media was bringing increasingly negative press. Barry observes, "I still felt it was an angle that didn't detract from what we were doing – I felt he brought it on himself because he wanted to. If you're playing games you've got to expect the ball to occasionally hit you on the nose. With hindsight I wonder how much of it spelled the beginning of the end in terms of loss of control and power." For Howard, the fact that this signalled to some extent the conclusion of his more confrontational interactions with the British media was because he no longer had the stomach for the games.

Amidst mixed album reviews, ironically, Magazine embarked on their most ambitious tour schedule to date playing large venues in Britain before setting off to Europe. Howard recalls, "Around the time of *Secondhand Daylight* we really went for it. We did a major tour playing major venues." Simple Minds were the support band and John Doyle adds, "The tour was really successful, breaking house records. Any negativity was quickly buried by the response to us live." He continues, "It's strange because I'm not a 'look at me' person. While I'm playing I imagine myself in the audience and as long as I please myself in the audience then I'm pleased with the performance."

Howard however, by this time, was finding a lot of the touring "tense, exhausting and repetitive". Although he was aware he had a certain presence on stage and that others found him charismatic, he says, "I read quite a lot of performers who say 'I only feel myself when I'm on stage'. These people must be people who love being looked at by a lot of people and love being the centre of attention and while that was true of me for a while there were other aspects of myself that didn't sit easily with that. I'm not in love with that in the same way some other people are."

Dave finds it hard to believe that Howard didn't really enjoy being up on stage. He argues, "He wouldn't have done those things if he didn't enjoy it. I mean, he would get into situations where he was rolling around the stage and just doing ridiculous things and really being very physical. I can never remember him coming off stage and not being completely drenched in sweat. You could argue that he was fighting that dislike of being on stage by taking it to an extreme. I think Howard has a definite innate showmanship – on his terms – and all that interview foolplay with journalists was all part of showmanship in a way. It's creating a character."

Although there was an inherent theatricality to the band's performances it stemmed from the music and the chemistry between the band members rather than elaborate sets. John Doyle describes Howard's performances as almost 'Brechtian' – a solo performance that couldn't happen without everything else that was going on around him, an ensemble piece but with a focal point. Sets were simplistic with a flat backdrop and minimal visuals. An exception was the gig at the Theatre Royal, Drury Lane where the band were approached to do something more ambitious. Accompanying the song *Big Dummy* a complicated and mechanised system of ropes, winches and pulleys dropped a set of 1930s' style suits from the ceiling and whirled them around the stage, arms and legs flailing. Dave recalls, "They cost a fortune, but they looked amazing!"

Around this time, Raf Edmonds was brought in as tour manager with Andrew Graham-Stewart taking more of a back seat. Andrew says, "Raf got on well with the band; they completely identified with him and he almost became the sixth member. They related to him and I wasn't so closely involved. I had other interests building." John elaborates, "Raf was very good at diffusing situations and pulling things on to himself. He was knowledgeable about a lot of things – he seemed to have done everything. He was somebody you could bat with but also use as a bit of a battering ram. He partied hard with us, but also had a good rapport with Howard."

Financially, however, the band was not as successful as the record company might have hoped for and certain tensions were beginning to surface. Record sales were down and touring was being undertaken at a loss. Howard says, "Some things got a bit financially out of control. I'd tried delegating responsibilities to Andrew." He quotes self-mockingly: "'Yes, I am the great star, the great talent. I've got great creative things to concern myself with – you take care of all that so I'm not troubled by it' – except it comes back to bite you on the ass very hard. I'm not saying he did anything wrong, I'm not saying he ripped us off, I'm not saying anything like that – but things got financially out of control in a way I wasn't happy with."

As Magazine and Andrew Graham-Stewart parted company, Raf Edmonds took over as full-time manager. Howard in particular found this period very stressful having chosen to shoulder the responsibility. He says, "Although Raf took some of the day to day strain, we – or rather more precisely I – retained ultimate financial control. That then added a lot of strain to me from that point on. Magazine never made a lot of money therefore it was always tight and a fight to make it work and stumble along and because I was keeping a hand on the reins I had to deal with that all the time. You end up with a sense of responsibility about things which some people are equipped to deal with and others are not very well equipped to deal with. And I, in certain ways, am not very well equipped to deal with."

Raf Edmonds already had a lot of experience in the sound, production and management side of the music business, both in the UK and US, working with a wide range of artists, including Alice Cooper. He moved back to New York during the emerging punk scene to manage Richard Hell and The Voidoids, who then toured with The Clash and Elvis Costello in the UK. A great fan of the live scene, he was excited to be able to take Magazine to America for their first full-blown Stateside tour.

Dave recalls, "That tour was one of the most exciting things I've ever done in my life. The pure adrenaline – it was like the last gang in town on a mission to convert these Americans. It was just a total buzz and everyone had a great time!" Barry agrees, "I really enjoyed it – it was a fantastic way to see America. I enjoyed going into a town not as a tourist but as part of the working fabric of the town. I felt at ease to mingle and not feel like an outsider. The travel was great and the performances were the icing on the cake. It didn't feel like a chore or a slog."

The tour took in the west and east coast of America with a sprinkling of gigs in the mid-west. Although not well known outside the larger cities they met with critical acclaim and according to Raf were considered "very hip". In New York they aroused the interest of people at the cutting edge of fashion trends and figures such as Andy Warhol and Nico put in an appearance at their gigs. In the middle of August, the band played Armadillo World Headquarters

USA Tour, 1979

Petrol station carpark, Sheffield, USA Tour, 1979

Press interviews, outside Virgin's offices, 1980

in Texas and John recalls, "That was the hottest place ever! It didn't have any walls – just a roof – and it was populated by what appeared to be Vietnamese war veterans. It was a great atmosphere but probably 110 degrees!"

The band travelled round America in a car and a van, communicating by CB radio. An over riding memory is of driving through Arizona to San Diego when the car broke down in the desert. John tells the story: "We were stuck for about eight hours with one bottle of beer between us. We had CB but nobody was willing to stop to help six blokes in a car. The crew drove past and didn't see us. Eventually we were advised to push the car to the top of a hill and coast down to the next town. What they didn't say was that there was a dry riverbed at the bottom with a bridge across it. We came to a stop halfway across."

He continues, "It was getting late and we'd been there for about five hours. Eventually an English man came on the CB. He was in a two-seater MGB, towing a boat through the desert. Raf and Howard got in the boat and got a lift to the next town – which was called Sheffield – and they got someone out to tow the car. By then it was the dead of night and it was literally a one-horse town. The hotel was closed so we spent the night in the petrol station car park watching a cockroach party. In the morning all you could hear were strange noises blowing the tumbleweed."

The American tour, Howard's personal experiences towards the end of this period and the critical response to *Secondhand Daylight* brought about a sea change and marked a watershed in terms of the band's dynamics and creative direction. The album was certainly unfashionable, with music too clearly independent of prevailing popular styles for most reviewers of the time to stomach. Dave says, "In some ways I don't know where it came from – I don't think anyone saw it coming – that's why it got a mixed reaction." Writing in 2000, Dave Simpson argues, "At the time, the absence of conventional song structures would confuse and disappoint a few reviewers. Years on it becomes clear that this is one reason why *Secondhand Daylight* was a masterpiece then, and remains one now."

Although media interest was still strong, this wasn't translating to record sales and members of the band had begun to become a little disheartened. Barry observes, "I guess in some ways a slight panic set in. I watched Howard begin to retreat. The band were now finding who they were which tipped the balance of him being the patriarch of the family and everyone bowing to his demands." Towards the end of this period, the band made the decision not to go on tour again until, as Howard said later, "one of the singles started doing something", continuing, "at this point we didn't seem to be any further on from where we were two years earlier." The next album was recorded under greater pressure.

Chapter Six —

My irritability keeps me alive and kicking …

The Correct Use Of Soap

MAGAZINE'S APPROACH to songwriting essentially remained the same over the course of the albums with Howard, Barry, Dave and John McGeoch bringing ideas along to the rehearsal studios, which would then be worked on as a band. Usually the music would come first and then Howard would work lyrical ideas around it. Whilst Howard came up with many of the musical ideas for *Real Life*, by the time they came to record third album, *The Correct Use Of Soap*, the rest of the band were making a much more significant contribution and in fact all members were given equal writing credits. The album was recorded at various times at Summa Studios (using the Manor Mobile), The Townhouse, Advision, and Britannia Row, with Martin Hannett at the helm.

Talking about the beginning of the process, Howard remembers, "I went back to the States for a holiday. While I was away the four of them started rehearsing. I remember talking to Raf on the phone and him saying, 'Yeah, yeah, yeah... they're all rehearsing, writing stuff. Don't worry – you stay as long as you want.' I went – 'They're writing? What? Without me? I'd better get back!' It was either very good psychology or he just meant what he said. It did act as a little bit of a spur to not prolong my holiday! When I came back they'd written four or five tunes – what would become *Philadelphia*, *Because You're Frightened*, *I Want To Burn Again* and possibly *Model Worker*. They were just instrumental pieces. In some ways I never knew quite who they originated with – although pretty obviously *Philadelphia* and *Because You're Frightened* would be John McGeoch. So that hadn't quite happened before."

John Doyle explains, "Things grew organically. Somebody would play something that would inspire somebody to do something else. In effect it was putting the Magazine sound on the bare bones of each song and creating a 'sound picture'. The aural image is one of the lasting things about Magazine's music." He says, "As I remember it, John was quite adamant that it should be more of a group affair. I certainly didn't write anything musical, however my input was treated as just as important. If John hadn't been so adamant I don't think that would have happened. It certainly avoided some things and allowed the songs to be freer in their construction." Dave adds, "It was much more a case of all of us in the same room writing tunes, on this one. The decision to be more democratic informed the way we wrote. Everyone would develop it and it was worked on in the rehearsal room until it became a song."

Howard reveals that a lot of things changed after the American tour. "Going to America in itself had a huge impact on me. But I'd been pushed to my limits before that – the whole getting rid of Andrew Graham-Stewart three weeks before the tour was appallingly stressful. I really thought I was going insane. Because of the financial position he'd got us into we had to do a renegotiation on our original contract with Virgin. We had to commit to more albums to get more money. You can't be totally straight with people, you know you're going to have to fire somebody, you've got an imminent tour of America when the furthest you've been in your life is Germany. I'd be discussing it with everybody but it was ultimately down to me to deal with it."

Because Howard was taking a much more active role in the business side of the group he felt that his area of control shifted away from artistic things to other considerations. He concedes that for the third album, the writing happened in a slightly different way. He elaborates, "Essentially I arranged the material – perhaps not solely. When I got back from America there were four bits of music but without much form to it. Still somebody had to make a song with it. That's what I did. I can't think of an occasion when I handed them the words and somebody went away and came back with the music. Much more the other way round or sometimes I had a bit of music to go with the words." He explains his position: "I remember Thom Yorke saying [about Radiohead], 'We're like the United Nations Security Council and I'm the United States.' It's kind of like that with Magazine. All the guys are pushing their ideas – especially Dave and John. A lot of the time the United States was taking a diplomatic role, not an assertive role."

For Barry, the fact that John McGeoch in particular was voicing more democratic ideas was not necessarily a positive step. He says, "I remember John being quite bolshie and everyone thinking, 'That's great – more credit' etc but I empathised with Howard. I have a clear picture of the look on Howard's face and his discomfort. He was like, 'Sure – if that's what you want...' and he was up for things being equal, but I felt it was a heavy blow for him. I felt he turned slightly away. I'm probably contradicting my actions at the time – I was probably right in there as much as everyone else, but I did think, 'It's not going to work the same any more.' There's something about someone having a clear vision and for me that was diluted. I thought it was wrong that Howard stopped fighting. For me, some of the Magazine identity got lost." He adds, "It's also quite frustrating when tracks are credited to everyone... before it was quite clear which sections I wrote."

Rather than diluted, Howard maintains that his vision was more complemented by everybody, including the ideas for the album artwork. He says, "I can't deny that it's a more communal effort. I think *The Correct Use Of Soap* is our best album so it certainly worked for me. Dave concurs, "I think some of Howard's strongest lyrics are on that album, so it's rather that he perhaps felt some relief – the pressure was off."

In fact, it's Howard's own view that he took a deliberate step back. He says, "One part of the shift was the change in me after my father's death at the end of the American tour. I didn't have much appetite for doing press or anything for a long time. When it came round to promoting the album, the rest of the band did quite a lot of interviews." He also says, "It was around this time that I stopped wearing make-up. I decided to be more 'real'. Artifice takes energy and I just didn't have that sort of energy or inclination any more. As part of that we decided not to have our pictures on the record sleeves this time round – not that we'd done it hugely."

One of the first songs written for the album, *A Song From Under The Floorboards*, was also one of the most communally written. Howard says, "I had a couple of chords then John had his thing, then I remember Dave suggesting adding the extra chord in the verse and the rising synthesiser phrase. The arrangement was very tight." John recalls working on the drum riff in the middle eight: "It was a pattern I was working on to the extent I was driving Dave round the bend because I kept playing it and trying to develop it into something else." Howard is open about the fact that the first line of the song was lifted almost directly from Dostoevsky's short story *Notes From Underground* and even put a credit on the single release to that effect.

Lyrically, Howard was again bringing to his writing personal experiences and feelings, as well as broader global issues, which captured his interest. Speaking of the song *Because You're Frightened* he says, "I was suffering a lot of fear then … I had to deal with, on a personal level, of hearing by phone from my mother that my father had died. That was in San Diego at the end of a long exhausting drive from Texas. And then two or three days later falling in love as deeply as I ever have and trying to make sense of that when I got back to Britain. Laura bought the book *Of Love and Lust* by Theodore Reik. One of the big ideas in that was that you fall in love at times of crisis in your life and that seemed to make an awful lot of sense to me. I combined it with the old Zen line of suffering being caused by craving."

One of the most personal songs on the album was *You Never Knew Me*. Barry describes it as a very odd but beautiful song that doesn't really belong there. He says, "The writing on that song is genius – right on the button." Howard recalls, "I remember strumming a few chords and playing that to them and I was probably so hesitant John was going, 'Can you sing a bit louder Howard, I can't hear you.' He came up with the guitar line that sewed the whole thing together. That was quite a lot about my relationship with Laura – and she sang on it! She had her own angle on it – she could make sense of it in her own way."

The experience of travelling whilst in the group afforded Howard a much broader palette of ideas to draw on and a basis for casting things in a slightly more international context. He says, "At a personal level big things had happened to me and you just start seeing the world more apocolyptically – the Soviet Union moving into Afghanistan, American hostages in Iran. Dylan had done his first Christian album which was very apocolyptically tinged." Many of the lyrical references in *Because You're Frightened* and *Model Worker* also reflect Howard's continuing interest in China.

Howard used the images around him to explore the same themes and preoccupations from earlier songs in different ways. He procured the phrase 'mother nature ripped me off' from an advert for rust preventative treatment and used it in the song *Philadelphia* ("which conveniently rhymed with healthier!"). Referring to a reference in *I Want To Burn Again* he says, "I think we passed a sign for 'Story Town'. That song has a very simple sentiment and conveys a little of the feeling of turning up at US immigration at that time – in those days it wasn't made very easy to get into the country."

Continuing to explore the theme of power, Howard became more interested in politics and global finance. He says, "The phrase 'sweetheart contract' would have come out of that. I had some stuff I'd got from some Soviet propaganda newspaper that used to come out fortnightly. The phrase 'standard issue sofas' came from a phrase in there. A little meditation on global power, showing just how paranoid and scared I was about all kinds of things." He continues, "The last song that was completed was *I'm A Party* and I remember Raf saying to me: 'All this hurt!' Life's like that sometimes."

John Doyle reveals that when it came to record *I'm A Party* the band inadvertently acquired a guest musician. He relates the story: "The saxophone part that John was doing was fine, but then the guy who owned the studio said 'Oh, just a minute, I'll ring Raf.' We thought he meant our manager. About half an hour later, this guy turned up. It was Raf Ravenscroft – the guy who played the sax solo on *Baker Street* – he took over. He came in, did it, and disappeared again!"

There is a general consensus that for this album there was a more conscious effort to push John McGeoch to the fore and to give him more space to develop his guitar parts. Howard says, "The guitar and keyboards are natural rivals – and especially in the case of Magazine with musicians like Dave and John. *Secondhand Daylight* was Dave laying it on quite thick – John had allowed himself to be squeezed out. That album had met with quite a negative reaction so it was natural to think, 'What can we change?'" Of the decision to tip the balance in favour of the guitar, Barry says, "We could probably smell John's departure. He had a very sensitive ego. I remember him having a real fucking go at me for the camera being on me during *Shot By Both Sides* on *Top of the Pops* – like it was my fault!" Howard adds, "It's not like John was a shrinking violet ...he could be quite forceful."

In retrospect, John Doyle feels that *The Correct Use Of Soap* had more of a guitar feel but not necessarily more guitar. He says, "There was not a lot of guitar on *Model Worker*. Maybe the overall sound is more guitar orientated – sharp, hard, short sounds as opposed to luxurious, mellow rounded sounds – which is what *Secondhand Daylight* was in comparison." Recorded off the back of the American tour, John considers that some of the album's dance feel was influenced by what the band were listening to at the time – Herbie Hancock, Parliament, jazz, Motown, Bowie's three 'Berlin' albums and a lot of dub and reggae. Dave agrees, "I think John and Barry became a substantially good rhythm section on that album – bass and drums. It got more refined. There's quite a lot of subtle funk on that album."

Out of step with the others in the group, Barry Adamson has reservations about their third album, maintaining that the production sounds dated. He says, "I didn't like *The Correct Use Of Soap*! Horror of horrors because I loved Martin Hannett, but I didn't like what he did with that record. It was too trebly – like he was trying to make it sound like the other groups he was working with and to me that wasn't our sound. Everyone disagreed with me but I wish those songs were done in different ways." The band can't remember why they turned to Martin to produce the album but he was well known to them having worked with individuals from the band in the past – most notably Howard on *Spiral Scratch*.

Additionally, Magazine worked with him, before the American tour, on a couple of tracks. Howard says, "We went into the Townhouse [Virgin's studio in Shepherds Bush] and that's where we started the alternative version of *The Light Pours Out Of Me*." The band also worked on '*Thank You*' with him, taking a copy of what they thought at the time was just a rough mix. In fact when they listened back to it later, as the album was nearing completion, it became clear that further honing was unnecessary – the action of Barry "whacking the snare drum up in the mix" had served to pull the whole thing together. Howard smiles, "John's got percussive noises on the guitar in there – you can hear the sound of his flanger – a shushing noise. I came in one day and Martin had got the engineer to clean off all this noise. I said, 'Where's the sweeping noise of the flanger?' He said, 'Well, it was noise so I got rid of it.' 'No – that's all part of it!' so back it came."

The figure of Martin Hannett has been mythologised over time; the image one has is of a genius or 'mad professor' obsessed with gadgets and the pursuit of the perfect sound production with just the right amount of resonance and reverb. Stories abound of the lengths he would go to in order to meet these ends. He would insist on multiple takes in order to give himself the greatest amount of choice when it came to editing and mixing the tracks. According to the former members of Joy Division he would attempt to unsettle musicians with the aim of extracting an optimum performance from them. Derek Bramwood of Strawberry Studios has been reported as saying that you could take a band that had got on brilliantly for twenty years, put them in a studio with

Martin Hannett and within five minutes they would be at each others throats. It almost seems as if Martin preferred to work alone in the studio without any perceived 'interference' from the bands he was producing.

Barry does allow that Martin could be a bit of a control freak, but that the extent to which he tried to exert control varied. He recalls, "Mood was a big part of it. Sometimes you'd walk in and there would be this sullen shut down shape. When we did the version of *The Light Pours Out Of Me* with him I worked out this step sequence – oscillation – on a moog. He thought it was good so we put it in to begin the track. I thought I was having a real say in how things were going. McGeoch had done this beautiful sax part and I said to Martin, "Are we going to drop the sax in now?" And he turned round and screamed at me, "There are no fucking saxophones on this record!" I realised that what he was doing was trying to hold on to a lot of ideas he was having and losing control."

However, on the whole, the nature of Magazine's working relationship with Martin differed from the reported experiences of some bands. Perhaps because they were old friends, perhaps because they were accomplished and confident musicians, the process was amicable and trouble-free with the band having a large influence over the final sound of the album. Dave says, "He never created tensions with us. I'd known him too long. He would never try that with me; he wouldn't want to. I think he really respected us. He said *The Correct Use Of Soap* was his favourite of the albums he'd worked on; that it was his best album."

Magazine appreciated the fact that Martin didn't have an establishment approach to producing; rather he was an inspirational producer who liked to improvise. Despite his array of gadgets, however, his technical know-how was not great, with John McGeoch joking at the time, "I don't think he can even spool a tape up". Howard claims, "Martin would not – I'd be tempted to say *could not* – function without a studio engineer. My experience was he was always whispering with the engineer as if he didn't want to us to know he didn't know what he was doing! That might be wildly unfair, but not a hundred percent unfair."

He continues, "I felt *The Correct Use Of Soap* was his best production in his career but it was with quite a lot of help from us. I would always have my hands on the mixing desk along with whoever the producer was. I always felt diplomatically and politically I was the most neutral point. If you got John on, the guitar would be loud. If you got Dave on, the keyboard would be loud. I felt I could take a slightly objective view along with the producer, although I had my limitations – I'm not very good with tone. When it comes to balancing a track – which is in some ways just finishing off the arrangement – that's one of the things I do. With mixing '*Soap*' it was a nice straight mixing board and I could get at it with Martin."

Despite Barry's concerns, the production of the album was roundly praised on its release along with the singles which preceded it. Lynden Barber wrote: "Hannett has stamped his personal approach all over the singles. For example, on stage *Thank You* is filled out with slabs of funky cheap-toned organ but on record Hannett has opted for a more sparse sound. The B-sides are interesting too – a new version of *The Light Pours Out Of Me* with drumming that sounds like it was recorded on the assembly line at Longbridge, and *Twenty Years Ago*, a chugging excursion in PiL territory based on a 'jam' between Barry Adamson and John Doyle."

Lynn Hanna wrote in *NME*: "Martin Hannett has matched Magazine's skill with their new-found freshness so that they've never sounded more fulfilled. And Devoto's voyeuristic attitude to his own growth makes the album a vivid examination of a mind in which sensation is synonymous with analysis and the shedding of inhibitions an event which merits meticulous attention. The album is an attempt to breathe a less-rarefied air and break out of the precious atmosphere that had almost stifled them. It comes in a simple sleeve, the songs have uncontrived titles, and Magazine have at last made an album that is personal rather than a conscious projection of a calculated persona. *The Correct Use Of Soap* is Magazine's masterpiece."

The most unlikely plaudits however came from the improbable source of Dave McCullough's pen. He wrote: "*The Correct Use Of Soap* is from any aspect a magnificent record – a brilliantly rounded and complete set of songs that marginally clarify the Devoto myths and at the same time establish many more ghosts and spirits for the curious." He finishes with, "I used to want to hit Howard Devoto. Now I want to hug him. He angers me. He keeps me awake. He gets under my skin at times still – and that's good. He's changed – I've changed. He's alive and kicking – so am I. Welcome to the world again Howard."

In the run up to the album's release, Magazine put out three singles within a month of each other: *A Song From Under The Floorboards*, *Thank You (Falettin Me Be Mice Elf Agin)* and *Upside Down*. Howard explains, "The idea was to release the whole album as singles and to release them at monthly intervals. Right at the end of the process they would all be collected together on an album. That would have been commercially stupid! Virgin made pretensions of going along with it. They were all going to be cardboard sleeves all with a different coloured label. That got screwed up very early on because somehow or other either Virgin or Malcolm Garrett managed to duplicate the maroon colour on '*Floorboards*' – *Sweetheart Contract* came out with a very similar colour."

Sweetheart Contract wasn't in fact just a single but part of a 12-inch or double 7-inch package coupled with live tracks recorded at The Russell Club. Intended as much as anything to announce the band's return after a short period

away from the limelight, the promotional campaign back-fired a little as reviewers were suspicious of the ploy. Dave McCullough, in a return to form,
drew attention to "Virgin's mega-packaging" writing: "For their next album-
culled 45 expect a track packaged with copies of every Human League album –
a free curry (as rec. by Howard of course) – two large bathroom towels ('Sopa'
– geddit?) and a blown-up life-size model doll of the now old and grey-haired
Mrs Devoto."

Howard recalls, "I'm sure Simon [Draper] started telling me protestations
were coming from the promotions department. They'd hardly got time to start
promoting something then the next single came along." Dave makes a similar
point: "I'm sure if we had stuck with '*Floorboards*' we could have at least got
into the top 50, because it was just starting to pick up radio play." At the time,
the band found it difficult to pinpoint which of their tracks would be more
commercially successful and Howard muses, "I don't think we had any perception of what would have made the best single. '*Floorboards*' did not shine out
to us as the single. Again – we used to be rather frustrated with Virgin because
we wanted more feedback."

At a time when Magazine were struggling to make any commercial headway
with the release of *Secondhand Daylight* and subsequently *The Correct Use Of
Soap*, three of the band found themselves in a position where the prospect of
commercial success came largely unsolicited. By mid 1979, most of the band
had relocated to London and John McGeoch, Barry and Dave were mixing in
more exotic circles. The Blitz night club, with DJ Rusty Egan, was central to
the dawning of the New Romantic era which embraced such bands as Duran
Duran, Depeche Mode and Culture Club. It became a regular haunt for John
and to a lesser extent Dave and Barry. When the idea to form Visage came
about, with Steve Strange as the frontman, they were intrigued enough to get
involved.

Dave explains, "Rusty approached John and said they didn't have enough
music to play on club night – there was a shortage of electronic synth based
music. It was suggested that we get together to make music for the club. It was
all very low key. We recorded the first single *Tar* on Genetic Records and things
developed to the point where we could make an album. When we all had a
gap where we could record we went to Martin Rushent's place in Walton-on-
Thames. Shortly after, he went bankrupt and Genetic folded. As far as I knew,
the album never came out and we went back to Magazine and forgot about
it. The next thing I heard was, I was walking through Soho and a member of
the management company that had picked up the album [Polydor] called over
and said, 'Do you know – you're number one in Germany?' We started getting
these sheets saying we'd sold hundreds of thousands of singles…"

Dave maintains that the whole thing was something of a joke and he certainly never entertained any thoughts of leaving Magazine. Financially it was

very lucrative for himself and John, but for Barry the whole episode left a bitter taste. Raf, who was initially involved in the plans to put Visage together explains, "Because we were the Magazine posse, the bulk energy would be Magazine. I expected to be involved in the managing side but it didn't happen like that. Chris Morrison managed. I saw it was going out of control of anything to do with me. Unbeknownst to me the infighting began. I spent a lot of time talking to Barry about it – he was extremely upset. He felt he was getting pushed out."

Barry says, "I watched Dave go off with the Visage people. I used to go to Blitz and I got drawn into the whole 'if you're not into fashion you're not anything mate'. We had this idea that we'd do this thing and it would be a gentlemen's agreement. I did a little bit of it but I'd walked away from it so I was suddenly out of the gentlemen's agreement. I held on to this idea that I was part of it – when I wasn't really. I was having terrible problems by then – I'd started on a slippery slope... I was looking for financial gain but I played it all wrong and only got paid for a couple of sessions." He reveals, "I was bitter about this for years because I got it completely wrong. It's not that long ago that I let it all go and came to terms with it."

Howard and John Doyle didn't get as involved in the Blitz scene. Reflecting on Visage, Howard says, "I don't think it concerned me in as this might be a threat to the very existence of the band. I think it more concerned me – what would the effect be on the *perception* of Magazine. It was all a bit pop and light weight and 'fashiony'. However it didn't affect anything Magazine were doing."

As well as occupying himself with the Visage project, John McGeoch was increasingly spending his social time rubbing shoulders with other London-based musicians including the members of Siouxsie and The Banshees. When, in late 1979, The Banshees were looking for a replacement guitarist for John McKay they openly courted John. Speaking to BBC Radio 2 for the *Spellbound* programme Steve Severin said, "I saw Magazine on TV doing *The Light Pours Out Of Me* and that's the moment when I just thought 'It's got to be him.' It just so happened that John had already been moonlighting a little bit from Magazine by doing the stuff with Visage. So he was bit of a maverick gun for hire anyway."

Over the next six months John worked with Siouxsie and The Banshees whenever he had downtime from Magazine and in March 1980 he made his live debut with the band. Deciding whether to stay with The Banshees or go back to Magazine was one of the most uncomfortable choices that he had ever had to make. Initially he chose Magazine and rejoined them for their UK and European tour in mid 1980. But Siouxsie and The Banshees slowly worked on him and eventually made him an offer he couldn't refuse. As Steve Severin said, "Banshees were a mistress and eventually we got him to leave his wife."

Speaking to the *Record Mirror* in 1985 John said of leaving Magazine, "It was very difficult to execute. It became very difficult to get out. I was leaving them in the lurch a bit so there was an incredible feeling of guilt. But I knew I had to take the bull by the horns and leave." In another article attributed to journalist Betty Page he discussed his departure further. He said, "The major reasons why I left Magazine really are private but it's hard to say because it's only after months of thought that I've realised the things that were niggling me. In Magazine everyone was a really good musician – with very strong ideas – and some of the frustration I felt came from the fact that concepts I had for songs weren't turning out as I'd envisaged them – and a few incidents happened on the road that I disagreed with."

He continued, "I was thinking well – should I give it all up when Siouxsie's manager called me up. They had *Happy House* written except for the guitar part so I worked with them and found it rewarding to play with different people like I had with Visage. The third Magazine album was my favourite – it was more guitar orientated than before; I had a lot of say on it but I had a kind of suspicion – there was a pendulous movement going on in Magazine's music and I was worried that the next album was going to be keyboard orientated – or whatever. I was by no means the leader of Magazine – Howard was all the way – but Dave and I were very close friends. That was one of the most difficult things about leaving – although there was a certain amount of competition between keyboard and guitar."

Reflecting on John's decision to leave the band, the members of Magazine point to his ambition and his frustration with the band's lack of success. John Doyle says, "John wanted, demanded, more success – commercial success. I don't think he thought it was the fault of us as a band but he felt the support wasn't there, the exposure wasn't there and he knew he could get it elsewhere. He was very driven, very ambitious. He had an offer – it was a career move. That's the best way to describe it." Barry adds, "There were disappointments all round that we weren't suddenly huge by the end of *Secondhand Daylight* – even more so by end of '*Soap*'. I can see how he would think, 'I'd better get over there then'."

It seems that one of John's main frustrations stemmed from Howard's attitude towards the press and the fact that he felt that this wasn't really helping Magazine's cause. By his own admission Howard was going through a rather introverted stage and had retreated from promotional activities. Raf was privy to some of John's resentment. He says, "I spent a lot of time holding John in. He used to get very upset and pissed off and he started hitting the Bordeaux, the claret. (He always reminded me of a Scottish squire – very studied – he would sit there with a bottle of red and discuss things.)"

He continues, "Journalists always wanted to speak to Howard. And Howard being so wounded that he was reticent to talk to them. Meanwhile the band

Rehearsals, with John McGeoch, at Summa Studios, Lots Road. This photo shoot was subsequently repeated with Robin Simon on guitar for the cover of *Play* (see page 163).

had grown in themselves and out of that I would always direct the journalists to the others. But the press still wanted Howard – I was in the middle trying to keep the press happy. I got involved trying to rescue the situation and keep them positive." Elaborating he says, "I remember a particularly traumatic time – being in Paris and the press wanted to talk to Howard and he didn't want to do it and I was putting forward John and he was getting very upset because the journalists didn't want to talk to him. It was all very hurtful."

At the time, the remaining members of Magazine had a rather philosophical attitude to John's departure. Howard says, "I don't think in my own mind I fully valued him. I did not think in terms of the business plan for Magazine for the next two years – it was much more fatalistic – 'Well if John wants to go, what can we do about it?' He didn't even talk to me when it came to leaving – he did it through Raf." In similar vein, John Doyle says, "We're all from Manchester. Dwelling on things was not something we did. It was like, 'Okay – sod it – next!' Our attitude was, 'Let's just get on with it.'" Barry has no memory of any discussions with John or anyone else about events and says, "All I remember is sitting in the rehearsal room and Howard saying, 'We'd better get someone new.'"

That someone new turned out to be Robin Simon. Barry recalls, "I remember Howard being quite excited by this guy he'd seen in Ultravox. He had a similar thing to McGeoch. We got him in and he could play similar to Mc-Geoch – it was quite scary! We thought, 'Wow this guy could fill his boots with his white boy outsider 'indie' look.'" Robin says, "I'd seen Magazine on *The Old Grey Whistle Test* and thought they were great. John McGeoch was one of my favourite guitarists. I'd just come back from New York and left my gear with Ultravox. Magazine helped me out and John gave me his guitar. He was an inspiration to me."

The band rehearsed the new line-up for a few weeks and then undertook a month long tour of America before moving on to New Zealand and Australia. Howard, who had got a lot out of the first American tour was especially happy to return. He says, "I remember when we landed at the airport, Barry saying to me 'Stop grinning so much'. Being back in America was still powerful medicine for me at that time." This time round the band flew rather than drove to most of their destinations taking in a total of fourteen cities throughout August. Tracks from their performance at Santa Monica were recorded for inclusion in the film *Urgh! A Music War.*

Australia was regarded as a new adventure although it was a gig in New Zealand that made the headlines. Somewhat behind the times, it was the only place where the band encountered skinheads who wrecked the gig causing major destruction. Sleepy Auckland then shut down for the weekend forcing the band to take their promoter up on his offer of a scenic drive out into the surrounding area. Once in Australia the tour picked up and the band played some powerful shows, sometimes sharing the bill with other bands.

John recalls, "We did some gigs with XTC and there was some banter in the press. Andy Partridge said watching Magazine was like watching a bunch of librarians. He said we may as well have been wearing white coats like scientists. There was a bit of a backlash and he regretted it. At one point we were sat in the foyer of the hotel and he came over and apologised and offered his ass for a kicking. All this malarkey in the press had passed us by and didn't bother us in the slightest so when he came over we more or less blanked him – it was like a double whammy! We knew we were powerful on stage because people told us."

En route to Adelaide the band missed a connecting flight; Raf and their Australian tour manager thought fast and procured them a small prop plane. John recounts, "It was the only way they could get us to the next place in time for the gig. But that meant it was a six-seater and it flew half the speed (or less) of a regular jet. When the plane didn't arrive the record company were making frantic phone calls between Australia and Britain thinking we'd crashed. We were having a great time flying at a height you could see Australia – just us and the pilot. It was a brilliant experience and we got there just in time for the gig."

It was whilst on this tour that the material for the band's live album *Play* was recorded. The record was made up of material recorded at the Festival Hall in Melbourne and mixed in London. A few overdubs were done in the studio after – mainly to repair sound difficulties caused by technical problems such as Dave's synth going off completely during *Parade*. Unlike many live albums this one had the merit of actually capturing the band at their best and John was particularly pleased with the track *Twenty Years Ago*. He says, "That song doesn't have a structure. It was always designed to be free form and sometimes it could fall apart. So to actually pull that off live really well and to get it on vinyl sounding like anywhere near approaching what it could be it was quite an achievement."

Continuing with his newfound love for Magazine, Dave McCullough gave the album five stars in his review for *Sounds,* describing *Play* as "magnificent". He wrote of *Give Me Everything*: "A fitting opener and a song, like a few others here, that suddenly makes me aware of the great sexuality in Magazine's music and particularly Devoto's lyrics." Of Robin Simon's involvement he wrote, "We needn't have worried. Simon's contributions, much harder and terser even than McGeoch's, come out of *Play* second only to Dave Formula's, whose keyboard playing is nothing short of inspired on the night. Together with Simon on the right speaker and Formula weaving his way across from the left they make a hard relentless sound that is much more competitive than Magazine have been in the past. It's almost as if Simon is fighting it out to prove himself and he's having a hard time against an on-form Formula."

Magazine played one final gig in Berlin and then returned home to begin writing for the next record. It was at this point that it became clear that replacing John McGeoch was going to be harder than they had thought and by the time *Play* was released in December 1980 Robin and Magazine had parted company. Howard says, "Robin could do John's stuff but he never seemed to come up with anything new. It was fine while we were on tour, but then it was more of a problem when it came to the fourth album. It was a problem we never quite resolved." John Doyle says, "Robin wasn't very extrovert. He was very insular. So from that point of view I think that's where it ended because of the type of person he was. There wasn't a togetherness with him – he just did his gig and that was it. I don't know if he felt there would have been a tomorrow but he didn't put out enough for there to be a tomorrow."

On leaving, Robin issued a formal statement saying that during his time with Magazine the two parties had "failed to achieve a genuine and practical basis for collaboration" whilst Magazine countered with "We found it necessary to seek a replacement because we felt a lack of the kind of personal commitment for creative communication that we require." Looking back, Robin feels that to some extent he "froze up and sabotaged his own gig". He says, "I felt a bit restricted stepping into John's shoes and was a bit concerned recording the live album that I lacked the originality of what I'd done before. I tried to leave the guitar parts alone a bit so that it was classic Magazine and just tried to enjoy it. In time I would have added more of myself." Referring to the time he spent with the band working on new material he says, "I didn't know whether to give my ideas to them – or walk out. I began to think it would be good to work on John Foxx's solo album and the chance came up at the same time."

Magazine never really recovered from the departure of John McGeoch. Certainly Dave felt his loss on a personal as well as professional level and says, "The dynamic and atmosphere in the band had changed. It was a massive wrench when John wasn't there anymore." There was a sense of frustration that John had left following the release of *The Correct Use Of Soap,* which most of the band felt was their definitive and best album. Dave says, "There was a great feeling making that album; the mood was much more buoyant." John Doyle agrees, "We were a unit. The chemistry was working. If we'd all stayed together the album after that would have been built on that. The musicality would have been more honed. It would have been something quite special."

Frustration also stemmed from the fact that commercial success and wider recognition was continuing to elude them. At the time Howard said, "Certainly we want to sell more records. We feel our potential is at least equal to a lot of people who exist and flourish better than we do." But tellingly, in the same interview with *NME* he also said, "What really counts is how far you bend to achieve that."

Magazine were not calculating, didn't tour incessantly and didn't always conform to the usual modus operandi of the accepted rock structure. Howard placed a high value on his privacy and disliked dealing with the press. Reflecting now, Dave says, "In the scheme of things I don't know if we would have become more successful anyway. We were a little too odd in a lot of ways to have ever crossed over into the mainstream."

Reflecting back, Simon Draper says, "There was still quite a strong element of my being a fan at that time and trusting in their judgement. Probably after *The Correct Use Of Soap* – when that wasn't successful I slightly lost confidence in their ability to be successful quite frankly. I do feel as we went along that Howard's own physical presence and the sound and tone of his voice and everything else – you started to realise that this was not pop fodder and in a way he was a slight barrier to commercial success." He continues, "I remember when we were contemplating signing Simple Minds thinking to myself why do we want Simple Minds – they're not as good as Magazine and we couldn't make Magazine successful. But Jim Kerr had more sex appeal is basically what I'm saying. In the end they were nothing like as good as Magazine but they were much more successful."

Dave argues, "That time wasn't ready for someone like Howard – another example of Magazine being a little bit ahead of their time. We weren't a con-

ventional looking band. Simple Minds were able to convert what they were doing into a theatrical presentation that leant itself to a stadium presence – they
cottoned on to the fact that to do that you have to get more anthemic. Which
they did. Jim Kerr saw what U2 had done and traced the template. Magazine
would never have been able to do that without a ridiculously obvious smirk
on their face. I can't take that stuff seriously even though there's an art in it –
there's a craft in it. It's the bombast – I can't take that bombast."

Simon Draper concludes, "There was definitely a feeling by the time of *The
Correct Use Of Soap* that the band had shot their bolt. *The Correct Use Of Soap*
was as good as they could get it and that didn't sell so what do we do now?"
What it meant was that Magazine entered 1981 as journalist Lynne Hanna
noted "shunted into a comfortably sized cult status – a slightly rarified side
line position that they may even have given the impression of enjoying". Although feeling no lack of creative success they were minus a guitar player, with
a lead singer who was (unbeknownst to the rest of the band) harbouring serious doubts about whether he really wanted to continue and a record company
who, although supportive, were becoming increasingly nervous about less
than spectacular record sales.

The stage set for The Correct Use Of Soap Tour

Chapter Seven —

A chain of
events,
*a change of
heart …*

Magic, Murder And The Weather

TOWARDS THE END of 1980 Magazine embarked on their second set of auditions for a new guitarist in the space of six months. Once more a series of musicians visited their rehearsal space at Summa Studios in Lots Road.

John Clay was one guitarist who responded to the advert in the music press and was given an audition. He recounts, "I was asked to learn three songs in preparation – *The Light Pours Out Of Me, A Song From Under The Floorboards* and one other. The band were pretty uncommunicative except for Dave Formula, but it seemed to go well and I was asked to return the following week. The second audition was a different affair altogether. Initially for a couple of hours there was just me, Dave Formula and Barry Adamson doing loose structured jams. Eventually John Doyle arrived and finally halfway through the day Howard Devoto.

"Whilst musically the day went well I kept getting the feeling that things weren't right within the band who weren't communicating with each other. At the end of the day we all decanted to a pub on the Kings Road in Chelsea where they explained their plans for a new album and world tour in 1981. Their manager Raf finally took me on a tour of his friend's hi fi speaker factory and to his flat, where he loaded me up with an armful of Magazine 12-inch vinyls and rarities, together with a cassette of demos for *Magic, Murder And The Weather* featuring Robin Simon, telling me that they would be in touch."

Auditions continued along with rehearsals, without a decision being made, and eventually musician, and friend of Howard's, Ben Mandelson arrived to help out. Ben says, "There was a point at which they got fed up with the auditions and decided to go with me." Ben inherited the band's guitar ("a rather fancy Yamaha!") then got his own guitars into commission again, all the time working his way through the band's repertoire and John McGeoch's parts. He says, "It was very kind of Howard to invite me to do it – he didn't have to – maybe he felt it would be more relaxed."

Howard admits now, "Ben was a fall back. I think I knew it was unlikely Ben would turn out to be the right kind of guitarist in the long run. In terms of getting an album together that would end up going in an interesting, different kind of direction – he would definitely have something to contribute to that. He was very different to John McGeoch. John worked his parts out and that was a large part of what the guitarist did. Ben was more improvisational. It did take him quite a bit of time to come up with what we were looking for – some of which we did try to incorporate. John Doyle adds, "Ben was definitely more eclectic; he had his violin as well which brought something to it. He had the element of spontaneity and his influences brought a bit of Africa to us, which wasn't there before."

For Barry the whole situation was symptomatic of the way things were going in the band. He says, "I wasn't that happy with the Ben Mandelson set up. I thought, 'How does this work? This guy who plays freeform jazz sort of stuff – can't play heavy chords, doesn't do feedback – doesn't even smoke cigarettes, let alone anything else. What's going on?' We were clutching at straws." It's probably fair to say however that by this time Barry's focus was slipping with regard to Magazine. Whilst in Australia he had become involved with, and was hugely impressed by, a set of musicians from Melbourne who would go on to become The Birthday Party and he says, "I was getting a bit fed up with how contained Magazine were, how controlled. I felt myself being pulled into a much darker place and that felt exciting."

Nevertheless the band set to work on the songs that would become the album *Magic, Murder And The Weather,* described latterly by Dave as "like the Curate's egg – good in parts". Reflecting on how he felt at the time Dave says, "It *did* feel different – I didn't totally believe in the songs while we were recording. It was as if things had shifted and it was never going to be quite the same. There was almost a languidness about it – you knew how to do it so you did it – it was almost a bit too easy to do. Had there been the same spirit there, there would have been the same vital and dynamic approach to it." Barry agrees and although he describes the song *The Honeymoon Killers* as "a great track – old school Magazine", for most of the others he says, "We were basically flogging dead horses. There was the inevitability of the end looming."

Lyrically, *Come Alive* was inspired by Howard reading of the Chinese mistranslation of the Pepsi-Cola slogan 'Come Alive with Pepsi' into 'Pepsi-Cola brings your ancestors back from the dead'. Other reading led to Howard using prison imagery in *The Great Man's Secrets*. He says, "Looking back from this venerable age I am now I can't quite understand the interest one had in violent crime and murderers... I read *The Executioners Song* – an utterly amazing book, *In Cold Blood* and watched films like *Badlands*. I look back now and wonder, 'What's so interesting about all that?' I don't understand it."

In an attempt to rescue some tracks, the band played around with percussive elements. Ben recalls, "There was one strange very atmospheric one where we had the classic untutored 'right everybody into the vocal booth with a box of percussion and rattle' which Howard liked – but which I would be horrified to do these days because I understand now how to work with percussion. But it got the job done." Speaking of the track, *The Great Man's Secrets*, Howard says, "A classic thing you do in a studio is to cut everything except one part. We tried cutting everything but the percussion just to see what it would sound like. We did it and I remember somebody saying – 'it sounds like Chicago'. That killed that idea dead! The same technique was used with *Naked Eye*. I felt I rescued that track as it was going nowhere. We cut the music off and left the drums and made it work."

Although the band were clearly struggling by this point, Ben Mandelson thoroughly enjoyed recording the album. He says, "I was quite innocent. There were all sorts of dynamics in the band, which I didn't really pick up on as much as a more perceptive person may have done. I was quite young and selfish and interested in playing the guitar and it was just a fantastic experience. It was the first LP I'd ever made. I'm sure now with my viewpoint as a record producer I was probably a nightmare as a young inexperienced musician but I did my best and I liked it very much."

He continues, "Although in terms of art rock Magazine were a very highly regarded, creative, quite risk taking band, at that point they were quite mainstream compared to what I was doing. I was coming from a background of weird folk and squeaking, playing toy instruments and rolling around on the floor. There were some tracks where I was definitely playing as out as I'd ever played but I had to get a bit more of a rock pop discipline for Magazine. I had certain rules to follow in the sense that the band had a sonic image and therefore it was appropriate for me to try and do it."

Most of the recording was done at Trident Studios with some additional work done on the Virgin barge in Little Venice. Ben says, "Trident had a classic echo chamber which was a room upstairs – a concreted whitewashed room with an array of speakers and an array of microphones. You could play stuff back and pick it up on different speakers so there was a physical delay time – nobody would use them these days but they sounded wonderful. Effects wise I had a delay pedal and the band compressor, which I inherited from John. Then there were the handclaps! Bands do that for a bonding experience. If you're a producer and you want the band to kind of feel together you say 'great idea guys – everyone into the stairwell, lets get lots of mics out', and everybody feels really happy."

Having worked with John Brand, on the live album *Play,* Magazine decided, this time around, to stick with the same producer for the new album. Although the band were quite happy with John's technical ability and there was no animosity, John Doyle says, "It just didn't work at the end of the day. We started off thinking, 'Oh – it'll be all right', but then the feeling built and it reached a point where we had to do something. Possibly what was not there from him was a passion – it could be that he didn't like what we were doing – maybe he thought it wasn't working." Dave was especially uncomfortable and hated the rough mixes John was doing. He says, "It got to the point where I got the impression he was going to be quite intractable about what he'd done, not wanting to change it particularly."

Rationalising it, Ben says, "In my experience as a producer now things that seemed *desperately* important to the band at the time, now it's sometimes quite hard to work out why you felt that. But the point is that you feel it – and making a record is an emotional experience." Howard says, "I don't think the dissatisfaction came from me. I think I was so locked up in my own issues of thinking this was going to be the last album. Also for me the problems with the album were nothing to do with the producer – the problem *is:* John McGeoch's gone and we haven't found the right replacement. The state of mind I was in then I was just getting worse. I was just crumbling. It was confirming all my fears about where the band might or might not be going."

He continues, "To our eternal shame it was actually Ben who sacked John Brand. We called him in for a meeting – because we always tried to be brave and if possible tell people to their faces. (I hope we didn't call him all the way in from his home in the suburbs or the minor counties just to sack him!) We were all there, including Ben, which shows how much he was involved in the band and again to me it shows just how weak I'd got... we were all 'umming' and 'aahing' and skating around the subject. Suddenly Ben just comes out and says, 'John – we just wanted to say we're finishing with you, we don't want you to finish the album.' It was like – 'Oh my God – Ben the new boy in the band who's only half in the band is the one who's had the guts to say it. Pathetic!'"

Ben remembers, "Afterwards Barry said to me, 'Blimey, you're a cold one – that's cold man!' I said, 'Not really – but we talked about it and this is our decision. Why not just say what we think?' So that was my little band moment and I was the new guy and maybe I transgressed all kinds of band dynamic lines but it had to be said. I'm actually not like that – I work as a producer and I know what its like to work with very sensitive artists and I've been an artist so I know what its like to work with sensitive producers."

The band then went back to the "old tried and tested Martin Hannett" and spent what John Doyle describes as a "mad, intense period" with him at Strawberry Studios in Stockport remixing the album. John says, "It was him taking the reins of something that was already recorded. Therefore it wasn't recorded the way he would have recorded it so there were some things that drove him around the bend that we had to repair. Imagine somebody bouncing off the walls physically – he'd go out of the room and come back hyper."

Additionally, according to Dave, Ben and Martin didn't see eye to eye, although Ben plays this down, "At Strawberry I discovered the joys of microwaves – I'd never seen those before – and I learned how to make cheese on toast with Lancashire cheese and coffee in the microwave. Technology was wild in those days! Martin changed some stuff and he moved some things around. I just used to do what I was told and maybe I had a couple of 'moodys' but basically I did my best to play what was necessary."

By this point Howard's sense of despair meant that he was taking more and more of a back seat. Of the decision to go back and work with Martin he says, "I'd lost so much willpower that the best I could manage was the diplomacy side of things. I'd not got a lot of willpower to have my own ideas and want to hold out for them and have a clear vision of things. I felt, 'Okay – if this is what it's going to take to get the album finished and keep everyone reasonably happy, then lets just go with it." Howard's lack of inspiration even stretched to the naming of the album and he says, "I was having problems with sequencing and coming up with a title. I remember we were in my flat trying to come up with something and we went round and round and round. Eventually, Barry said to me, 'Well, what's the album about, Howard?' I said, 'Magic, murder and the weather,' and he looked back at me quizzically, kind of with a raised eyebrow, as if to say, 'Well, there's the title then...'"

Looking back now, the band insist they had no idea at the time of the depth of Howard's unhappiness. He says, "I'm sure that by the beginning of the serious recording of 'Magic' I was sure in my own mind that I would not be going on at all after the recording of the album was completed. I don't think the others picked up on it. I was determined it wouldn't affect my creative efforts on the album to the degree that I almost went overboard with my work for it. I didn't want to tour and I think it was impossible to imagine the band staying together without playing live. I think in some ways the whole process with writing and recording 'Magic' just consolidated and confirmed my thinking. It was quite hard work and without John it just wasn't quite good enough."

The exact circumstances of Howard informing the band of his intention to leave are unclear as consciously or unconsciously each member has a different memory – or in the case of John Doyle, no memory at all. Whilst Barry remembers a very official meeting, Dave recalls finding out about it via a phone call whilst he and Barry were actually in Australia. Howard's journals tell this story:

> "'I have to quit.' I said. Relief carried me buoyant, out to sea. I had to say it individually to everyone, over the telephone. I don't think I could have said it to everyone assembled. I had tried – sort of – the previous two weeks. The first time I'd ended up warning everyone about the financial crunch to come, the second time I'd announced that I didn't want ever to do any gigs again. The following day *Magic Murder And The Weather* was cut at the Townhouse. We were all there."

Howard feels that there must have been further discussion about his decision when they met together in a café down the road from the Townhouse shortly after cutting the album. He says, "My only specific memory of that – either towards the end of that or as we were walking away towards the tube station – is of Barry kind of humorously turning to John and saying, 'Didn't you just want to say, 'You bastard!'"

He admits, "There was a degree of cold bloodedness to the timing of it. You've done the record, you get your money for it. If you stop there you're not too bad. Everybody can have a little bit of money and you haven't gone off potentially losing it all touring." To the press he announced, "I feel that a change for me has been long overdue. I could have held on for another six months but I didn't want to tour to promote the album. I don't whole-heartedly dislike performing but I don't like long tours and their ever-decreasing returns." It was left to Raf to deal with the record company's reaction.

Howard's overriding feeling was one of tremendous relief, tempered by quite a bit of guilt. Although he hadn't previously conveyed his feelings to the group, he reveals now that there were some signposts during the recording of the final album. He says, "There were little notes of finality. For the album I managed to bag the Virgin catalogue number that was one hundred on from *Real Life*. And the graphic on the album is from our first official gig – the Bruce Gilden photo from Mardi Gras. It was coming full-circle, book-ending it."

Speaking of the burden of responsibility he felt overall to the group he says, "It's entirely of significance to me – and perhaps to me only – that the last track on the last Magazine album fades out with the words, 'I am responsible'. It was a little part of my thinking when track listing." Dave reflects, "In the end it weighed too heavily on him. Yes – he took too much on. He took a lot of the weight. He didn't need to do that – other people would have taken some of the responsibility but because of the personality he was it was just part of him. By the time he'd done it for a certain amount of time the press just didn't want to see anyone else. In a way he'd created his own burden."

Raf concurs, "He was the one everyone wanted to get to. He was the one who always had to talk to the press. Criticism made him retreat and he didn't really want to talk to anyone unless he felt there was an empathy." He continues, "Howard is very sensitive and intellectualises everything. He was inspired to be in a band but when he got into it he realised that – particularly as a frontman – you're putting yourself up for an awful lot of stick – and an awful lot of effort. He had to psyche himself up to go on stage. I do remember sometimes asking him to go back on and he wouldn't – the band got pretty hairy about that sometimes and felt a bit embarrassed."

For Ben there was a great deal of disappointment that the band had literally come to the end of the road. He says, "I was looking forward to touring and I was curious to see how it would work." On reflection, the band feel that they could have handled the break up a bit better. John admits, "There was a certain amount of Manchester bravado – we don't give a toss. Here's the album. Looking back, we could have taken two years off – that would have been far better rather than making it a fait accompli. In our innocence that's what we did. We could even have shelved the record. That may have helped not just the band but some individuals as well." Barry took Howard's decision badly and reveals, "Three years ago, I was still furious – I don't feel like that anymore."

The whole band did feel some degree of frustration at not being able to play the new material with Dave saying, "If we don't play it it'll get up and play itself." They dismissed the idea of bringing in a new vocalist on the grounds that it would simply be a pale imitation and rejected the idea of a farewell gig as cheap nostalgia, with John rationalising, "Once you've rehearsed that much you may as well go out on the road." The press mourned the demise of the group with Ian Pye writing in *Melody Maker,* "The violent end of Magazine is totally appropriate to the style of a genuinely individual and provocative group." Meanwhile, speculation began as to the band members' next potential musical projects, with much of the attention naturally focused on Howard. As he took time out, Paul Morley wondered in the *NME* whether people would be prepared to wait. Howard replied, "Whoever said I was expecting them to? They either will or they won't."

Chapter Eight —

Somewhere else something else on my mind …

After The Fact

THE CORE MEMBERS of Magazine took some time out to consider their futures after Magazine eventually split in 1981, before picking up the threads of their musical careers. The musicians who played a more fleeting role in the band's history also went on to pursue a variety of successful and creative ventures.

On leaving Magazine, Martin Jackson took up sticks with another band who developed into one of the biggest cult bands going: The Chameleons. Later, tiring of drumming – and ironically considering his reservations about the direction of Magazine's sound – he developed an interest in keyboards and drum machines, working alongside Andy Cornell of A Certain Ratio. With Andy he recorded an album called *UK Electro* on a minor label, then with the addition of singer Corinne Drewery, Swing Out Sister was born. The band made the most of all the opportunities that came their way and achieved great commercial success. Martin says, "Once you get a singer involved everything tightens up a bit. The first single came out and sold about 800 copies, and then everything went crazy! I was with them five or six years; it was a bit of a scary experience!" Eventually, Martin made the decision to leave for a life of greater anonymity and settled in Hampshire where he continues to write and compose for different media.

Post-Magazine, Bob Dickinson initially pursued a career in teaching. In the 1980s however, he presented a number of systems-based musical pieces in gallery environments and initiated projects with artists from other disciplines. Through the influence of his then wife he became very interested in paganism and spirituality and during the 1990s he produced a series of what he describes as, "non-linear pieces of a ritualistic nature for performance in a variety of natural environments using a combination of natural and humanly-produced sound." His interest in rock-climbing also led to a greater empathy with nature and the environment and in 2001 his book *Music and the Earth Spirit* was published. This book examined the ways in which music and sound have been used in different cultures to connect with the 'earth spirit' and in some ways rekindled his own interest in avant-garde music. Although Bob now runs a degree course in music production with the University of Lincoln, he continues to compose what might be described as minimalistic, atmospheric music for renowned musicians across the globe.

From Magazine Paul Spencer joined pub rock band The Speedometors, recording one album for Acrobat/Arista. He then finished his drumming career with "a couple of fun-packed booze-ridden years" with The Alex Harvey Band. Since then, Paul has been involved in film working with U2, The Rolling Stones and other bands on their music videos. He moved to Hollywood with the intention of working his way into the movie business and was given the opportunity to direct television programmes. On his return to the UK Paul started his own music TV company producing and directing (mainly) music documentaries whilst still finding the time to run the Maverick Festival – an annual event near his home in Suffolk that celebrates Alt-Country and Americana.

Robin Simon left Magazine following their successful Australian tour and collaborated with John Foxx on albums between 1981 and 1986. In 1988 Robin was reunited with Billie Currie in Humania and in 1993 he joined Blitz, alongside his brother Paul, Sue Rachel and John Foxx. Robin and Paul formed AjantaMusic in 2003, after several years spent touring internationally and living on Ibiza, releasing the instrumental album *And Now We Dream* in 2005. In 2009, with vocalist Gina Watson, they released the second AjantaMusic album, *Above The Cloudline* (on which Dave Formula appears as a guest musician). Robin also guests on Dave Formula's solo album.

Although Ben had only been with Magazine a short while, he found himself embroiled in the dying embers of the group. He says, "While Howard was making his mind up about what he wanted to do I ended up in this theatre company as a musician doing a show about the life of Hank Williams. It was meant to be the concert he didn't get to – he died in Ohio on the way to Canton. The stage show was a mock-up fantasy of 'What if he made it to the concert?'" Because Ben had signed a publishing deal whilst with Magazine he had the funds to undertake a trip to Nairobi soaking up the African music, which was to influence much of his later work.

On returning to London, Ben played rhythm guitar with African band Orchestra Jazira. Then came a stint with satirical world music band 3 Mustaphas 3 whilst leading a parallel life working for a record label called Ace records, looking after their world music label GlobeStyle Records. Between 1991 and 1998 rather than playing himself, Ben was producing bands; for a number of years he was also the director of the annual Womex conference on world, roots, folk, ethnic, traditional and local music, with whom he is still involved.

He resumed playing in 1999 when Billy Bragg asked him to help put together a band to do the Woody Guthrie project. Ben was delighted to be able to incorporate his many and varied traditional and folk instruments, including hybrid instruments of his own invention, such as the barizouki and resozouki. He is a prolific and well-respected producer, especially in the field of world music, and continues to collaborate and perform with different musicians around the world. His latest collaboration with Lu Edmonds and Justin Adams (collectively Les Triaboliques) resulted in the album *Rivermudtwilight* released in 2009.

After drifting away from Magazine in 1980 and dabbling in various side-projects, John McGeoch joined Siouxsie and The Banshees as a full-time member at the beginning of their most creative and successful phase. Speaking some years later, John said, "I was surprised to get the call. They invited me along to their rehearsal studio in Camden and within two days, we'd routined *Happy House*. They really liked that guitar line; that was the clincher. I was going through a picky phase, as opposed to strumming. *Happy House* was lighter and had more musicality in it. They invited me to join. I was sad leaving Magazine but The Banshees were so interesting and it felt like a good move."

The second single he played on with The Banshees was *Christine*. Speaking on the Radio 2 documentary *Spellbound*, Steve Severin said, "I think every other guitarist has absolutely failed miserably to find that first chord of *Christine*. It's a McGeoch chord, and nobody else knows what it is." John in fact played guitar on what are widely considered to be the best three Banshees' albums – *Kaleidoscope*, *Juju*, and *A Kiss In The Dreamhouse*. For many, his work on the 1981 album, *Juju*, is some of his most memorable and outstanding playing. According to Siouxsie Sioux, "John McGeoch was my favourite guitarist of all time. He was into sound in an almost abstract way. I loved the fact that I could say, 'I want this to sound like a horse falling off a cliff', and he would know exactly what I meant. He was easily, without a shadow of a doubt, the most creative guitarist The Banshees ever had."

However, John's three-year sojourn with The Banshees effectively came to a messy and very public end in 1982 when, apparently struggling with alcohol and stress related problems, he collapsed on stage in Madrid. Siouxsie recalled to *Spellbound*, "After the second song, I realised from the set-list he was playing the wrong songs to what everyone else was playing and I just remember looking at him, and he was looking at me going 'What?' And I just thought, 'Oh, no, no, no, no, no, no, no.'" John himself recalled later, "I really ruined a gig in Madrid in October and that was it basically. I was definitely out of control. I was having a hard time coping with the demands of it all. I had a bit of a burn out, that's the easiest way to sum it up. I ended up in hospital and I didn't get a second chance. By the time I'd got myself sorted out, it was a done deal." John left The Banshees in November 1982.

John's friend Joe Barry maintains that John's mental health had always been relatively fragile. He says, "I didn't think he was happy in 'Siouxsie' – but he'd almost stopped being happy – he was quite low and depressive. He was drinking and taking a lot of coke." John Doyle says, "John was always a hedonist – his reason for doing something was purely because he could. Not for anything more altruistic. The opportunities that were open to him which led him to indulge in the more hedonist libertine excessive side of his character are what did for him in all senses of the word." He continues, "He was always down to earth. If he saw a need for something and he could fulfil it – why not. He would and could talk to anyone. Not in a condescending way he would just help – he was that sort of bloke." Joe concurs, "He had enormous generosity of spirit – he was beside himself with joy that I was doing a law degree."

John picked himself up and after a short spell in Scandinavia producing, he joined his old friends and former Skids members Richard Jobson and Russell Webb in the band The Armoury Show. With the addition of John Doyle to the line-up they released the album *Waiting For The Floods* in 1985. Despite financial input from John by way of his royalties from his time in The Banshees, and extensive backing from management company Q-Time in the push for success, the band didn't survive beyond the first album. John Doyle reflects, "There were plenty of heavy rock riffs. We honed it and did produce some good music of that period. It was probably a case of trying too hard."

Fortunately for John McGeoch, John Lydon had been trying to recruit John as Public Image Limited guitarist since 1983 and finally got his man in 1986. He became their longest serving member staying with them until they effectively (but not officially) disbanded in 1992. Together with Allan Dias he became the backbone of the new re-invented PiL, contributing co-writing and acting as a full member. His arrival helped change the whole sound and outlook of the band; with a more guitar friendly 'rockier' sound becoming the way forward. For some, he transformed PiL from a left field, experimental outfit into a provocative, marauding rock band.

A more settled (and some would say vastly under-rated) line-up paid dividends for the band and saw them releasing a new studio album *Happy?* followed by *9* and *That What Is Not*. It also led to them touring extensively, building a whole new following. Despite having an unfortunate baptism when he was hit in the face with a full two litre bottle of wine at a gig in Vienna in 1986, John toured with them until their final shows in September 1992.

During this period, John had been based in LA, but now moved back to London and attempted to put together a variety of musical projects, which largely failed to get off the ground. He formed a group called Pacific with Spandau Ballet's John Keeble, but with the exception of one London showcase little else came of the venture. Turning his back on the music business for a while he began training to be a nurse, but this wasn't pursued and he again tried to pick up the threads of his musical career, writing background music and theme tunes for TV. His daughter Emily recalls that by this time he had left most of his rock stuff behind and was playing classical music and Beatles' songs at home for pleasure.

On 5 March 2004, John died at home in his sleep. Speaking on *Spellbound*, Malcolm Garrett said, "We should remember him for what he was – one of the finest guitarists of his generation. I mean, the whole thing about where he originated – punk was not about guitar heroes, you know – The Clash said, 'No more guitar heroes'. But the point was he was a guitar hero at a time of no guitar heroes. That's how we should remember him. His recorded works are timeless and that's the best that anyone can hope for in this life – to leave something that will live forever."

Following Magazine John Doyle had a short-lived liaison with Barry in the guise of Provocative Agents. Wanting to make an impact, they were aiming for a more commercial sound with the help of a female singer but although they made some headway with publishing and promotion the project never really got off the ground. In 1981 John collaborated with Ken Lockie (Cowboys International), contributing drums to his solo album *The Impossible*. Further collaborations followed with artists as diverse as French opera singer Armande Altai and Japanese musician Akira Mitake. The latter collaboration came about as a result of John's work with Barry on the Magazine track *Vigilance* which was much admired – although Barry was asked to join the project he eventually dropped out leaving John to work with Norman Watt-Roy instead.

John then had a brief flirtation with the world of acting. This direction wasn't pursued however and in 1983 he found himself reunited with a former band mate again – on this occasion John McGeoch in the briefly successful Armoury Show. By this time, former Magazine manager Raf was working with Pete Shelley and subsequently John found himself asked to tour Pete's solo album for a year or so. Continuing their collaboration, John and Pete worked together on some music for the film *Some Kind Of Wonderful*. Ventures with other bands didn't work out, so for family reasons John eventually returned to the world of 'proper work', developing a career in graphic design and desk-top publishing and pursuing music purely as a hobby.

Whilst in Australia during the latter part of Magazine, Barry had found himself increasingly drawn to the social and creative scene in Melbourne. Post-punk band The Birthday Party, with a creative core of Nick Cave, Mick Harvey and Rowland S. Howard, were integral to this scene with their dark, challenging brand of rock. When in 1982 bassist Tracy Pew was jailed for a time, Barry was asked to deputise. This led to him joining Nick Cave's next band, The Bad Seeds, as a founder member and recording four albums with them.

Of the period 1983 to 1988, Barry says, "Despite being in the throws of an exciting and highly creative new beginning, in myself I was beginning to get scarily lost – as a result of trying to push myself way beyond my limitations." Speaking of his time with The Bad Seeds he says, "Some of it was amazing – onstage telepathy and doing stuff that you haven't rehearsed, making art as you go along." However, Barry found what he refers to as the "enforced negativity" hard – a negativity that was necessary to " lead the art into a darker conclusion". Through a process of self-infliction, he perceived himself as the outsider, driving himself harder and further into a corner he would find difficult to get out of as a result. He returned to Manchester to be hit with news of a family tragedy, which would see his sister die within two weeks.

Barry left The Bad Seeds in 1986. As was the case whilst he was with Magazine, Barry had spent some of his time in the band obsessively creating his own music on the side and he left with the realisation that what he wanted to write about was on his own doorstep. Recognising his potential, Mute offered him a solo deal in 1987, resulting in the 1988 single *The Man With The Golden Arm* – the first indication of the cinematic direction Barry was to take up with his solo career. But it was *Moss Side Story* that channelled Barry's influences and obsessions into an autobiographical soundtrack for a film that didn't exist outside of Barry's head. Speaking at the time, he said, "I had all these scenes in my head and I was putting imaginary music to them so I thought... why not? It's also a different approach to making an LP."

Although continuing to work creatively, the downward spiral, which had begun towards the end of his time with Magazine, was compounded by the loss of both of his parents within a very short space of time. The isolated existence he'd become almost comically known for in The Bad Seeds, was now a more painful reality than it had ever been. Eventually, through what he describes as "a total surrender of lifestyle and choices" he dragged himself back from the brink one night. He reveals, "I had one almighty epiphany... there I was, staring death in the face again and next thing it was like watching the towel being thrown in and finally knowing in myself that it was over; that it was okay to stop fighting and be led from the ring. I'd kind of lost but won at the same time."

The next twenty years saw him focused and concentrating on his solo career. Following the release of *Delusion* in 1991, he released the Mercury Prize nominated *Soul Murder* – an album which has been described as a confessional psychic journey. The music from this was later used by Trent Reznor and formed part of the soundtrack for *Natural Born Killers*. Time spent in Los Angeles producing the band Ethyl Meatplow gave rise to several ideas, which went into the six track hit *The Negro Inside Me* (1993) – according to *Rolling Stone,* "an upbeat celebration of mixed blood, interracial love and the release of something passionate".

The desire to delve further into films led to Barry studying the medium in New York and it was here that Barry formulated the ideas for his next album. Following painful hip reconstruction surgery, he released what he has described as the third part in a personal trilogy – *Oedipus Schmoedipus* in 1996. *Rolling Stone* wrote, "Adamson can brilliantly – and without words – suggest entire movie scenes with dizzying combinations of dance beats, jazz phrases, finger-snapping big-band arrangements, luscious strings and even references to 60s French pop."

This album led to widespread acclaim as Barry was recognised as an innovative composer with vision and insight. It came to the attention of David Lynch who offered him work on the score for his forthcoming film, *The Lost*. In the next ten years, Barry scored music for television – including the BBC drama *City Central* – and released a further six albums including *As Above, So Below* in 1998. This album featured Barry's vocal talents, and for the first time in over ten years he began performing live with a full band. According to reviewers, his 2002 album *The King Of Nothing Hill* saw Barry radiating a new confidence.

In 2008, Barry released his most recent studio album, *Back To The Cat* but was keen to develop his interest in film. He says, "Writing and directing totally excites me! With my schooling in music and life and the amazing opportunities I have had so far to work with some of the best people around, I'm hoping that'll move into being able to make movies as the logical expression of a life lived on the edge of sometimes the abyss and sometimes a very plush cushion indeed!"

Following his decision to leave Magazine, Howard flirted with the idea of working with a female singer but the venture came to nothing. He spent the remainder of 1981 putting together a primitive 4-track recording facility and writing and demoing songs. A contract was negotiated with Virgin and he continued working on the tracks which would eventually form part of his first solo album. He continued his interest in American politics by undertaking an evening class in the subject and took a holiday with his then girlfriend, Laura, in the American mid-west. The following year he continued writing and recording and he reflects, "Over the year, my relationship with Laura deteriorated and I wondered vaguely if I was provoking emotional crises just so I would have something to write about. *Jerky Versions Of The Dream* was the album that emerged, at that time, out of the continuing turmoil of my life."

The album was released by Virgin in 1983. Simon Draper admits that although the name Howard Devoto was still important to them – in the way that Morrissey later transcended The Smiths – there would probably have been less commitment in terms of marketing and promotion. With Dave Formula on keyboards the album delivered a couple of singles – but even the potentially commercial song *Rainy Season* made little impression on the charts and the album appealed largely to a cult following.

Having previously worked with Bernard Szajner on his album *Brute Reason*, Howard's first appearance on stage since Magazine's final gig was at the Lyric Theatre, Hammersmith in May 1983 alongside the avant-garde French composer. Reviewer Adam Sweeting wrote, "The moment most of the audience had been waiting for was the arrival of the enigmatic Howard Devoto who materialised for a couple of guest spots. Apart from anything else it was refreshing to hear a voice among the instrumentation – though Howard's lyrics were suitably opaque. Nonetheless he seemed to be enjoying himself – capering around his falsetto register with aplomb." Meanwhile, a solo tour was put together to support Howard's new album. Reflecting on that period, he says, "At the time, I survived. In retrospect it was all fucking awful. Over the course of a few months in 1983, tours of the UK, Europe and Scandinavia, and the USA were ... completed."

The initial relief which Howard had felt on making the enormous decision to quit Magazine – and tell the others of his decision – had by now dissipated and he says, "New anxieties instantly emerged to take the place of the old ones." Following the muted response to *Jerky Versions Of The Dream,* he saw little reason to continue trying to elevate himself from the cult status that seemed destined to be bestowed upon him and in a pattern that was to be repeated in the following years, stepped away from the world of music for a while. With friends (including Malcolm Garrett) he got involved in setting up a book production company but the collaboration was not a success. Discussing any possible regrets around that time he says, "Circa 1985 -86 I regretted everything, including being alive."

In 1986 he was tempted back to music as he says, "It felt like the only thing I had going for me. I'd got myself into a very bad hole and really, at that time for me, going back into music was like the thing I knew. I knew it was something I cared about immensely. I knew I could kind of hang on to it. It would preoccupy me, it would distract me, it would do all the things I needed to do, as well as hopefully provide me some subsistence." Howard was sure he didn't want to be part of a full-scale band again, but knew that he needed a collaborator. It was through Raf (who was still managing other bands including Buzzcocks) that Howard came into contact with Noko.

Howard and Noko began writing and recording together and then put a band together to play the *Festival of the 10th Summer* at Manchester's G-Mex stadium in July 1986, to commemorate the tenth anniversary of the Sex Pistols first playing in Manchester. They played a short set as Adultery, borrowing backline from The Smiths. (Noko also played a set with Pete Shelley at the same gig in a line-up that included John Doyle). Signing to Beggars Banquet in 1987 and deciding on the name Luxuria, Devoto and Noko released two LPs: *Unanswerable Lust* (1988) and *Beastbox* (1990) and toured Europe and the USA throughout 1988. The final UK Luxuria gig at the Town & Country Club (now The Forum) in London featured appearances by Barry Adamson playing bass on a rendition of *The Light Pours Out Of Me,* and Morrissey, who read a passage from Marcel Proust's *A La Recherche Du Temps Perdu.*

Howard says, "I thought, and still think, that *Beast Box* was a really great album. Far better than the first Luxuria album, worlds better than my solo album." The lack of interest with which it was received however led him to once more consider his position. He explained later, "I got out of the music business because I had to for my own sanity and life. It wasn't treating me very well by the end of the 1980s. It had taken me a while to recover myself, but I really thought *Beast Box* was a great album and the fact that it was so overlooked just made me feel, 'Okay, there's much more of you than there is of me, so you must be right and I must be wrong.' So I went and got myself a proper job, basically. Complete life change. I couldn't make a living anymore. I had to get real."

Throughout the 1990s, Howard worked as the manager of the archive at a leading photographic agency in central London. At the time he said, "It is only since I've done the job that I have a practical view of the future – and therefore a degree of – well – happiness. It is such a relief not having to rely for my survival on my creativity or lack of it. There is the thing about how – after what I was and what I might have been – I end up doing a job that can be seen as pretty boring. Well – I could never have worked in the music business. My pride would never have let me. Whatever I feel about not being involved in all that is far outweighed by the relief of not having to perform all the duties you're expected to if you want attention." (*Uncut*, October 2000)

Despite this, Howard continued to dip into the music world. He collaborated briefly with his Luxuria partner again on some tracks for Noko's new band Apollo 440. In the middle of the decade, Magazine fan and lead singer with Mansun, Paul Draper, got in touch. Paul takes up the story: "We had a mutual friend of a friend who told us Howard was still making demos and writing so we asked if it was possible to do a collaboration. To my surprise a package came through the post with a cassette tape and some sheets of lyrics. On the tape was a rough demo of *Railings,* which we immediately jumped on and a sheet of lyrics for *Everyone Must Win.* This was the stuff that stood out from everything else. I felt a pressure to do justice to the material but I can honestly say the hardcore Mansun fanbase still tell me to this day that they were two of the best tracks we ever did. *Everyone Must Win* became a live favourite of ours and the audience."

Describing the sessions, Paul continues, "Howard turned up one day at Olympic studios in Barnes which is now closed down. He was pretty quiet but we talked over music and what we liked then headed into the studio to play Howard where we were up to with his material. He liked it so we proceeded to do vocals on *Railings*. Howard sang it in the middle of a darkened room and I listened in the control room. It was all dark and quiet, late at night, and when Howard's voice came out through the speakers it was like 'wow' this guy's voice is still incredible! I remember feeling pretty small as when I did my take it showed how thin my voice was next to Howard's. You can hear that on the record. His phrasing of the words and emotion in the lyric was mesmerising – I felt like an amateur. We put the vocals together and edited it so it worked and

Howard sat in with Spike who was mixing it until we got the desired balance and emotion in the final mix of the song. A memorable night. Howard melted into the London night after that and I never saw him again..."

Although Howard was divorced from musical activity for much of the 1990s, he had sporadic contact with Pete Shelley. Raf was still managing Buzzcocks (and Pete) and the idea of Pete and Howard writing together was mooted – originally with the next Buzzcocks' album in mind. Howard says, "As Pete and I started working together more and more it became obvious the material wasn't suitable for Buzzcocks. The pair performed a short set in tandem at the ICA for a Mute Records evening in September 2000, introduced by Howard with the words, "He's Buzz and I'm ...." Initially intending to collaborate on just a few songs they ended up recording the electronically influenced album *Buzzkunst* releasing it exactly twenty-five years after *Spiral Scratch*, in 2002.

Raf suggests that there were plans to do more gigs but when it came to it "Howard couldn't go through with it." Pete says, "As far as me and Raf were concerned it was going to be me and Howard with some equipment, light show planned, we go on and we play. But he wanted to know everything that was happening at every point of the evening. He was doing it like it was choreographed like a ballet. With all best intentions, the more you try and make a big production out of it – it's like the Spinal Tap 'Henge' thing - everything can go wrong."

Pete continues, "And then he wanted to start taking my front room, where we recorded and mixed most of it, on tour. The idea for the stage set was I take my settee, computer table, big screen TV – we take that on the road and set that up on stage every night. But to me, the idea of Buzzkunst was that people

would be able to see me and Howard there, and people would be pleased to see Howard singing. We didn't have to do any act or anything. Anyway, that didn't happen much the disappointment of myself – and the record company."

Howard himself says, "That album was done on computers. Once it was completed, my line was always: 'If we're going to do any gigs, then Pete needs to formulate what he's going to be doing on stage.' My question was essentially: 'If we gig, I know what I'll be doing on stage, I'll be up on stage singing. So what's Pete going to be doing on stage while I'm singing?' I never got any answers. I had a full-time day job to be getting on with and didn't press the issue. Consequently there were no gigs."

Over the following years Howard started to write his memoirs but he is not sure if they will ever be published as a book. He says, "Spoken word was the idea for the years up to and including summer 1975 and my move to Salford. After that ... anything could happen." Eventually relinquishing the day job, he spent time travelling and pursuing his interest in philosophy whilst still continuing to write and record his own music. In July 2009, he was awarded an honorary doctorate from the University of Bolton.

As Magazine individually and collectively called it a day, Dave spent time in Australia then returned to Britain towards the end of 1981. He describes the following year as a "bit of a blank period" although he did some producing with London band Design For Living and worked with Visage on their third album. It was not a particularly happy time and a dispute over Dave's exact contribution led to a souring of his relationship with drummer Rusty Egan. A spell with Linder Sterling in the experimental jazz-punk band Ludus followed. Live performances were relatively rare, the most infamous being a show at The Hacienda in Manchester on 5 November 1982. On this occasion Linder used

her most confrontational tactics to express her sexual politics, decorating every table in the club with a paper plate holding a red-stained tampon and stubbed cigarette, later performing in a dress made of discarded chicken meat sewn into layers of black net. Dave reflects, "It was a considerable achievement in its own way, but I'll never forget Tony Wilson's face when he walked in."

In 1984, together with Alan Rankine of The Associates, Dave produced a single for Winston Tong of American cult band Tuxedomoon. Around the same time, interested in the mechanics of recording, he began to seriously pursue an idea that he'd harboured since the early 1970s – that of setting up his own recording studio. His idea became a reality when he was introduced to and then formed a partnership with Richard Boot who had both premises and some money. Dave sank the money he had earned from his recordings with Visage into the partnership and Strongroom Studios was born.

Located in Shoreditch it seemed an unlikely place for a studio to thrive, but Dave and Richard succeeded in making it into a unique and vibrant place, which was able to attract notable artists through its doors. Dave says, "We made a pact that we would never advertise it in *Melody Maker* – there were so many studios in there all trying to undercut each other. We wanted it to stand apart. We got a really nice Amek desk and Malcolm Garrett designed the colour scheme based on the vibrant colours of the EQ section of the Amek. I insisted we got a grand piano. There was a great acoustic in the recording area."

In its first year the studio facilitated debut albums from The Housemartins and Erasure plus albums from John Cale and Nico. Dave says, "Those four albums put us on the map straight away and covered lots of areas of music. We also recorded all the *Spitting Images* audio – it really took off." Dave also involved himself in smaller projects with young bands and co-produced the second Luxuria album *Beast Box*. Dave reveals, "During this time I turned down the chance to produce the first Stone Roses album. I knew their manager Gareth Evans and he was very persuasive. The band were massive in Manchester but nowhere else. I went to see them a few times but it seemed to me they had a certain attitude problem and I couldn't imagine working with them – we'd have fallen out!"

The success of the studio meant that they were able to open Strongroom 2 on the same complex. Dave and Richard also opened one of the first studios in London specifically designed for artists to compose and record with computers using the new technology, midi. After a few years this solitary way of working was beginning to lose some of its attraction for Dave as he preferred collaborating with musicians rather than computers. As the recession bit in 1989 forcing the closure of some studios, Richard proposed borrowing large amounts of money to make Strongroom bigger and ultimately more viable. At this point Dave decided to bow out because, as he says now, "Although it was a good time, I was becoming more of an administrator than a musician."

On relinquishing his share, he and his family sold their house and moved north to Lincolnshire where Dave immediately set about building his own studio, Red Bird, in his back garden. A phone call from an A&R man at EMI led to his collaboration with a young band called In Aura. Dave both recorded with them and undertook a tour with them supporting The Human League. A friendship with a local record shop owner and musician then led to Dave touring Europe and Japan with ironically named electronic band Stock, Hausen and Walkman.

In the mid 1990s the music work began to dry up a little and Dave says: "For the first time in my life I did some regular work." He began teaching at High Melton (part of Doncaster College) eventually leading a music technology course as well as working hard to improve facilities for the students and develop new recording studios. It was during his time there that he met up with musicians Andy Seward and Keith and Dave Angel. Dave joined forces with them in The Angel Brothers and their funk off-shoot The Finks, gradually doing less teaching and more music. The Angel Brothers fused musical cultures as diverse as Flamenco, British folk, New Orleans funk and Anglo-Asian sounds. They released two critically acclaimed albums, *Punjab To Pit Top* and *Forbidden Fruit,* and Dave was able to earn a living from his music once more. This enabled him to reverse out of teaching, eventually taking voluntary redundancy.

Dave's last outing with The Angel Brothers was at Womex, Seville in 2006. In January 2007 he began working on a solo album, recording at his own Red Bird Studios. Entitled *Satellite Sweetheart* it features over thirty guest musicians including past and present members of Magazine. Dave laughs, "It took me five months to persuade Howard to sing on *Via Sacre* – it was something he thought he'd left behind. I was fairly persistent. He liked what I'd sent him – so it was perhaps a matter of time. I bought him a USB mic that he could plug into his computer to record his vocals. He sent various versions, which I edited together and put back into the track. This process continued over a few weeks until we were both really happy with it – it's now one of the signature songs on the album."

It was whilst Dave was working on his album that he was sent some Visage tracks to remix. In a strange twist of fate he opened up one of the tracks and realised that the voice he was hearing was that of John McGeoch. Dave created the track *The Anti-Hero*, using John's voice with some piano, synthesiser and guitar. For the first time in nearly three decades, the voices, musical ideas and contributions of Dave Formula, Barry Adamson, John Doyle, John McGeoch and Howard Devoto were all to be heard on one record.

Chapter Nine —

The timing was right, but it was still a surprise …

Reunion

LTHOUGH THE INDIVIDUAL members of Magazine had worked separately with Dave on his solo album, the series of collaborations re-established lines of communication between them. It was as Dave was about halfway through the project that Manchester promoter and Magazine fan, Pod, got in touch with him via MySpace to enquire about his recent projects. After discussing Dave's solo album, Pod tentatively broached the subject of the possibility of Magazine themselves reforming to do some gigs.

Conscious of the fact that the band had tried to get back together three years previously and it hadn't quite worked out, Dave couldn't offer Pod any hope. But when the promoter came back with a serious, considered offer, Dave, Pod and Graeme Oxby (from management team Wire-Sound) held a series of meetings in Manchester to put a solid proposal together. Dave knew that the only way there was a chance of any gigs happening was to put something really concrete in front of the others. As a fan, Pod's motivation was to see the band, in his words, "given their rightful place" and he was prepared to make the conditions right for it to happen.

Whilst Dave and Barry had continued to pursue a musical career, Howard and John had largely left this behind in recent years. Howard admitted to having doubts and anxieties about the reunion whilst ruefully aknowledging that to have those was "in his job description". He was widely quoted in the press in the lead up to the gigs as saying, "Dave made me an offer I couldn't refuse. He said 'Howard, it's your last chance to be venerable.'" The fact that Howard had by this time given up his 'day job', and that there was a convincing management structure behind the proposals, meant that the idea of working together again as Magazine seemed a much more viable proposition.

The individual band members came together in September 2008 for a photoshoot, which Dave describes as being "a little bit edgy, naturally". At this early stage, John was still taking a cautious approach saying, "It's gonna happen or it won't. When it nearly came about three years ago it was as exciting; this time around I'm going to choose not to get excited until I'm on that stage. The music deserves to be heard – the buzz will be far greater than any financial gain."

For Barry, the fact that he'd found success as a solo artist was something that he had to consider when the idea to play together again was first seriously discussed. Reflecting, he says, "I have had a bit of trouble with it. I tend to leave things in the past. I've been doing music for twenty, thirty years only to go back. It's a bit like snakes and ladders. I'm not being judgemental – it's the way my mind and ego observes it: I'm on two rows before the end and I've thrown the dice, gone back to number two and I'm like eighteen again." However he was confident that it was the right thing to do as a band, saying, "We know it will work because we did a weekend three years ago. Even though we fought like cats and dogs, it sounded fantastic. It was like time had stood still – everybody was up for it."

As Barry, Dave and John came together to audition guitarists in October 2008, the feeling of rightness was confirmed with Barry enthusing after, "I felt quite connected with it. Which was a first really for me because I feel that progress is about striving for something new. But … I allowed myself to drop into it and I had a prophetic glimpse as to how an audience therefore might respond to what we're doing and it was really fabulous. I think it's going to be great. Music does something to gel space and time – not just gel but make it disappear. I can't believe that the same sequence of notes played by the same people can have such a profound effect. If we wrote that stuff today we wouldn't change a note. It would be still of the time – this time."

He reveals, "There was an incredible McGeoch moment when I was shocked again with how innovative he was. I remembered back to him in the studio when at the end of *Permafrost* he said, 'Just play the end again' and he turned the guitar one way and made a high note, then turned it the other way and it was like a police siren and he dubbed that on the end. When I listened to it at the time I thought, 'He's sketching out the terrain of where Howard's coming from.'"

Of the time spent in the studio with the others he says, "It was like going home. It's like when your parents ring you up and say they haven't seen you for a while and you get there and you go, 'Oh God, this is the last thing I need' … but then you open the fridge and you drop a bag of clothes down and they suddenly disappear somewhere. There's the TV and there's a familiar kind of toastiness. At the end I kissed the bass and said 'Welcome home.'"

The problem of who to bring in as guitarist was left up to Barry, John and Dave and following the auditions the decision to work with Noko was, according to them, a "no brainer". As well as being a John McGeoch afficianado and a talented musician in his own right, Noko was, and is, in some ways part of the extended Magazine family having worked with all members of the band individually in the interim years. When Howard was told of the decision he said, "I couldn't be more pleased."

Noko was delighted and says, "This was the band I always wanted to be in. I'd be here at these gigs even if I wasn't playing. This is such a big deal. As a guitar player I always had this connection with McGeoch and his sound – all the way through The Banshees – and it's kind of in my blood. I'd have been very disappointed if someone else had got this gig." He continues, "There were rumours in the press that it was going to be some Manchester superstar guest guitarist. I'd said to them, well basically I'm here – to quote Spinal Tap – someone already in the organisation! I didn't hear anything for six months! I'd kind of assumed they'd got somebody – it's going to be Johnny Marr, it's going to be Billy Duffy... And then the tickets went on sale and I thought 'Should I get myself some tickets?' Then I thought... 'I'm sure we'll be sorted for the guest list!'"

Eventually, Dave phoned up and invited Noko to attend auditions. Noko recalls, "I did my slot – it was a very strange experience! Of course I'd known them over the years so it was a loaded situation. I wasn't just walking into the room on a social basis. When I left the studio, after having played the songs – once, just once – one, two, three, four: *Shot By Both Sides*, one, two, three, four: *The Light Pours Out Of Me*... When I left that room I had no idea whether it had gone badly or well. They're quite laconic – they don't give a lot! I was just in this funny sort of daze. I went back to my studio and all the guys there were saying, 'How'd it go?' I was like, 'I don't know really...' I was just in a strange sort of trance – 'What did I just do there, what just happened then?' Dave phoned up later in the evening and said, 'Do you fancy doing it?' and the answer was obviously 'Yes!'"

Individually the members of Magazine prepared themselves by getting in the best physical and mental shape possible. In Howard's case, he did it: "Laboriously. Push-up by push-up, word by word and note by note. It had been a long, long time." Just before their February gigs in 2009, the band came together for a week's rehearsal. The natural apprehension that individuals might have felt on the first day was offset by, as John says, "the major trauma of actually trying to get there". The first day coincided with the worst snowfall in the south of England for many years and saw Howard and Dave trudging through the snow trying not to fall over, and John negotiating an almost standstill railway system ("'No trains' notice said 'Don't know, don't ask!'") while one member of the backline crew walked in from Brixton. For Barry the whole day had a surreal, magical edge as he struggled in to the rehearsal studio near London Bridge by car, with the radio station seemingly playing every record from 1977 to 1981.

Following some discussion with the others by email, Howard had put together the set list for the shows as well as a rehearsal schedule. He says, "After the amount of time we'd been absent, it had to be largely a 'best of' set. A 'best of' set with twists. Obviously we wanted to introduce some *Magic, Murder And The Weather* songs. It's not unlike sequencing an album." The decision to use Rosalie Cunningham and Samantha Valentine – from support band Ipso Facto – on some backing vocals, opened up the choice of tracks available. John says, "The original idea was to do '*Honeymoon Killers*' into '*Great Beautician*' but it didn't work. It made more sense to lop off the 4/4 part of '*Beautician*'. Howard treats the whole thing as a theatrical event with a beginning, middle and end. I was amazed by it – he spent a lot of time preparing it, he involved us and the whole thing fitted together very nicely."

The band made the decision to open with *The Light Pours Out Of Me* although Howard initially had reservations about this. Dave's enthusiastic assertion to him that it was a "showstopper" didn't help, but the band ultimately stuck with what John felt was a brave choice. The set was paced and the gravitas given to *The Book* with the introduction of the lectern added to the theatricality of the show.

The band were keen to remain faithful to the Magazine sound and actively sought out original instruments or ones which could replicate the sound as far as possible. John used a refurbished drum kit from the early 1980s and Dave's musician son, Max, helped him out by lending him a china cymbal. Max also helped Barry find an Ovation bass of the type he'd used on a lot of the songs in Magazine's early days. Dave used an original Yamaha SS30 string machine and says, "I didn't want to go down the route of using a computer – you can buy simulations as plug-ins for computer but I don't trust that – I would rather have the machine."

The Odyssey was a clever emulation of the original ARP, rebuilt by German company Creamware and Dave used a Hammond Suzuki SK3 – a digitalised version of the Hammond organ, still with the revolving Leslie speakers. He also used another keyboard, a Nord Electro 3, which had on it a Yamaha electric grand sound, which he had used originally. It also had the proper acoustic pianos as featured on *Parade*. Dave says, "We've had all those years' experience since, so you're going to play them differently, but why not use those instruments – they sounded good then so they'll sound good now."

Noko laughs, "When Dave first phoned me up he said, "Look – I know you've been playing Gretsch White Falcons – we can't have any of that, this is a Yamaha SG gig! And I was like, 'Yeah, okay, I understand the parameters of this!' Obviously it's all about repertoire – there's a Magazine legacy and there's a repertoire and it's about playing those to an audience that kind of expects things to be played in a certain way. But there's still latitude to personalise it. Each Magazine guitarist has done that. I think Robin did that in a way that hasn't been appreciated. I think he plays *Give Me Everything* better than John McGeoch ever did for instance. There's different takes on it. Ben has had his little bit on the aesthetics. All those guys made contributions."

He continues, "The irony of this is – up until a couple of years ago, Howard had John McGeoch's original Yamaha SG that they'd bought with their advance from Virgin in Manchester. I used to play it occasionally on some Luxuria stuff. He actually sold it – which is really annoying! It would have been nice..." He continues, "What I've done – on a purely geeky, technical

Magazine's reunion tour, February, 2009

LIGHT
MODEL WORKER
BEAUTICIAN / HONEYMOON
FRIGHTENED
YOU NEVER KNEW ME
RHYTHM of CRUELTY
BURN AGAIN
THIS POISON
FLOORBOARDS
PERMAFROST
BOOK
20 YEARS / DEFINITIVE GAZE

SHOT
THANK YOU
MOTORCADE
BIG DUMMY

level – because the repertoire demands a certain sound, I'm using a modern cleaned up version of what John used. I'm using the same guitars – all my guitars are Yamaha SG's from 1978 – 1979, which is what John used with the same Marshall amplifiers. I've got the exact original MXR flanger – it was certainly the one that was out on the *Play* tour and I think it might have been John's original one. The sound of Magazine is so much about the sound of the Yamaha SG into a MXR flanger into one of those Marshalls. There's minute changes of those flanger settings for every song. I've got a whole pile of paper on the floor – I've got settings for every song."

The band took to the stage for the first time in over twenty-eight years on Tuesday 10 February 2009 for a warm-up show in Oxford. Over the following seven days they played two dates at both Kentish Town Forum and Manchester Academy, punctuating these with the only Scottish gig at Glasgow's own Academy. Although the band were confident that the shows would be well received they were still taken aback by the audience's response. Barry says, "The ovation after *The Light Pours Out Of Me* was astonishing really. It was like a spontaneous celebration, not just of Magazine but of all kinds of stuff; validatory and affirming, feeding itself to us and then back to the audience. We were all dumbstruck every night." John reveals, "The immediate effect after the Oxford show was that we all hugged without giving it a second thought – and I'm not a huggy person. I was beaming! The whole event was more than I'd expected – I could not have forseen that reaction. After the first London show, I lay in bed giggling for about half-an-hour."

For Howard, who had struggled to find any enjoyment in being on stage in the early days, there was no comparison in terms of how he felt then and now. Speaking to the *Daily Record* before the Glasgow show he said, "I'm not saying I was allergic to enjoyment but it didn't come to me easily. It's a very different ball game at this stage in life." His confidence stemmed partly from the fact that the material was tried and tested by time and his evident pleasure showed in his relaxed stage performance. For the Ipso Facto girls, being on stage and singing with their idols was "insane" as Sam says, "It's a really surreal feeling. You almost feel like you're watching yourself, and you can't believe it's true..."

Every single person in the audience at the Oxford gig seemed to recognise that they were witnessing a special event. Audience members included Jonny Greenwood who wrote on Radiohead's website the following day: "Saw Magazine play last night in Oxford. It was remarkable ... nearly thirty years since they last played, and they were everything you could hope for. It was strangely free of nostalgia – just great songs, well played. The one mention of their past – a tribute to the memory of the remarkable musician John McGeoch – was very affecting, but also part of this sense they had of 'we know this music's great, you know it's great, and it goes like this' – nothing smug, or especially triumphant – it was just obvious to everyone there. They opened with *The*

Light Pours Out Of Me and didn't falter once."

The newspaper heavyweights were in attendance at the first Forum gig with *The Independent* giving it a 4 star rating – even though most of those in the know felt that the second night surpassed even this. Pete Paphides wrote, "Any fears that a 28-year layoff might have diminished the impact of Magazine's canon have been all but obliterated." He remarked, "Both the band and the crowd united in the realisation that no one expected it to be this much un-alloyed fun." In *The Guardian*, Alexis Petridis noted, "What's striking is not only that they sound fantastic, but how contemporary their 30-year-old material seems." He continued with, "It's hard not to think that this might have less to do with the fact that rock music has turned in Magazine's favour in recent years than with the fact that their records sounded unique and timeless to start with."

The enthusiasm with which the Glasgow audience welcomed the band easily matched the other shows and may even have eclipsed it. Writing in *The Herald*, Neil Cooper awarded the show 4 stars and wrote: "The missing link between Roxy Music and Radiohead, Howard Devoto's troupe of post-punk fabulists always understood the power of pure melodrama – and so it is with this second coming 28 years on. With a back-drop of a chalk-faced chorus by artist Linder Sterling, the band enters to the strains of *The Thin Air*, a majestic instrumental by the band's late guitarist, John McGeogh."

He continues, "It's a typically arch introduction to a 90-minute set of should've-been-hits, throughout which Devoto conducts the band the way a precocious two-year-old would. He updates a lyric in *Model Worker*, still the only love song to use the word 'hegemony', or reference Obama, and, on *Definitive Gaze*, swoops across the stage, arms outstretched like a bird. Most theatrical of all is when he leads Rosalie Cunningham of uber-bobbed support band Ipso Facto to the microphone for a bittersweet collision of two waltz-time songs, *The Great Beautician In The Sky* and *The Honeymoon Killers*."

Magazine have always maintained that their albums – and particularly *The Correct Use Of Soap* – were designed to have a timeless quality. Speaking to *The Herald*, Howard said, "Now, thirty years on, I feel fairly vindicated. We were quite young when we made it, but those songs don't feel like kids' stuff, and as I start to step back into them, they still seem to stand up." To *The Independent* he said, "Your time eventually comes around again, on the waltzers, the round-abouts. And when it comes, you've got to jump on. We wanted to remind people what we did then. And what we can do now. I don't have the same ambition. But I have a greater capacity for happiness."

Cautiously taking things 'one step at a time', the band played a second string of gigs in summer 2009 – taking in festivals in Spain (Benicassim), England (Latitude) and Ireland (Electric Picnic). Further one-off dates were slotted into the diary for the UK including a festival warm-up gig in Sheffield and dates in Manchester, Edinburgh and at the Royal Festival Hall, London. John acknowledges that the idea of writing new material is a "huge step" but tellingly the band have not ruled this out. Howard continues to stress that there is no master plan saying, "We'll take things as they come." The possibility remains of short tours taking place in 2010 in Europe, Australia and America with Barry saying, "I'd personally like everyone in the world who wants to see Magazine do just that, then put the bass back in the case."

Chapter Ten —

I know beauty
*and I know
a good thing
when I see it ...*

Artwork & Sleeve Design

PUNK ROCK – with its uncomplicated chord structures and rhetoric of shock and disruption – fitted perfectly with the cut and paste photomontage images that adorned much of its related artwork and fanzines. It was a time when musicians realised that they could control not just the music but the visual imagery of the band as well. Magazine took forward this attitude and worked to create record covers which reflected the innovative nature of their music. Speaking about the band's approach to their sleeve designs, and what they should communicate, Howards states, "It should say: 'great record, great band'. And say it subtly and, sometimes, not so subtly."

The two people outside Magazine who have been most involved in the band's artwork and record cover design are artist Linder Sterling and designer Malcolm Garrett. Both Linder and Malcolm were students at Manchester Polytechnic in the mid 1970s, along with Peter Saville, and between them they went on to define the graphics and visual literacy of the punk and post-punk period. Malcolm and Peter were also at school together. In an interview with *The Independent,* Peter said, "Malcolm and I would sit in our art class at Saint Ambrose, drawing and planning our future album covers together." All three moved in circles which brought them into contact with other artists and musicians (including Morrissey), with Linder eventually moving in with Howard Devoto.

Born Linda Mulvey in Liverpool in 1954, Linder spent her adolescence and much of her adult life in Manchester. Attending the second Sex Pistol's gig at the Lesser Free Trade Hall was a pivotal moment. She relates how the day unfolded, "I saw a white transit van drive past the Southern Cemetery in Chorlton, south Manchester. There was a poster stuck to the side of it which said: 'Malcolm McClaren's Sex Pistols' – and maybe other names too '...at the Lesser Free Trade Hall'. In my head I saw a collage of tartan, sex and violence, and so thought that it may break the monotony of the day to go along. No one that I knew had ever been to the Lesser Free Trade Hall. I didn't even know that it existed." This was the concert at which Linder first met Buzzcocks and Howard and she was later to say, "I walked into that concert with fate by my side and have only ever looked forward since."

Speaking of how she developed her individual creative style, she says, "By June 1976, I had become a little bored with drawing. Now, of course, I wish that I hadn't; I wish that I'd pushed through the boredom and taken my pencil somewhere new. I'd begun to experiment with collage; I used cut out elements from magazines, catalogues, the stuff that lay around me. At first, I kept the drawn line there too; then, the moment of liberation: pens and pencils were put away, the scalpel adopted, and progress was made."

Linder introduced Malcolm to Howard shortly after Buzzcocks had released *Spiral Scratch,* and subsequently to Richard Boon, a friend of Howard's and a Fine Art graduate from Reading University. Malcolm says, "Richard and Howard had assumed responsibility for managing Buzzcocks in the early part of 1977, and they asked me if I could design a poster for them that could be used to advertise one-off gigs – a sort of standalone poster that could be hand-written over with venue details etc. The design featured the first version of the Buzzcocks logo, and I hand printed a small number of posters, in college, in a variety of different colourways, some of which remarkably still survive."

When it came time to produce a sleeve for *Orgasm Addict,* after Buzzcocks signed to United Artists later that year, it was decided to use one of a series of Linder montages. Made in the bedroom of the Salford house she shared with Howard, Linder took images from traditional men's magazines and the fashion and domestic women's magazines of the era. She then made "these peculiar jigsaws", making a point about the cultural expectations of women and the treatment of the female body as a "site of commodification". A number of Linder's montages had been used on handbills for Buzzcocks throughout 1977 but the image chosen for *Orgasm Addict* famously depicts a naked 'glamour' girl with her head replaced by a household iron and nipples replaced by teeth.

Malcolm says, "Once the image had been selected, I handled the design and layout, and the physical production of the artwork. All of the typography was either typeset letter by letter, by hand, or stencilled using architects' lettering stencils. Because the sleeve was restricted to two colours I chose a dark colour which would render the image well, and a bright colour to complement it. I found that by photocopying the montage it gave it a more suitable texture for this type of two-colour printing. Photocopiers were quite rare at the time, but I had access to one which allowed me to scale the image to fit the 7-inch sleeve."

Malcolm was born in Northwich and studied typography and graphic communications at Reading University for a year before moving back to Manchester. He says, "I was always very interested in the shape of text and the meaning of words, or the distortion of the meaning of words through the use of typography – what typeface you choose and how you lay things out. If you look at *Another Music In A Different Kitchen* (first Buzzcocks' album) and *Orgasm Addict* I was very interested in breaking up the text into different planes, which to my mind suited both Buzzcocks and Magazine. Peter and Howard were both very lyrically driven – but in quite different ways. Peter's lyrics are fiendishly simple. I always think of him like P.G. Woodhouse – he writes volumes in one sentence, whereas Howard uses words playfully and appears to enjoy them in their own right. Abstruse is the word I used to describe it – in my head this is somewhere between abstract and obscure."

He continues, "I remember, right at the start, having a sketch book full of ideas for a Magazine logo. I remember one that had all the letters separated in odd groupings – the latest Radiohead logo reminds me a little of that. Mine just never made it out of the sketch book. I liked the way it was completely breaking up the syntax. I subscribed to a school of thought that tried to introduce a consistency of font but also tried to allow for a level of freedom – being able to go off at tangents. So you could maintain visual links but allow for fresh manoeuvres within the visual framework that you were adopting. The font for Magazine's record sleeves changed all the way through."

Malcolm worked once more with Linder on the cover design for Magazine's first single *Shot By Both Sides*. He says, "Linder and Howard chose the cover image. Linder was much more of an illustrator and I was more of a graphic designer. Linder was good with imagery and I was good at putting the whole thing together and making it work. I did the typography for the back of the single cover and put the whole thing together as a piece of artwork ready for print." As Malcolm explains, Odilon Redon was Howard's taste in imagery and he wanted something as far removed from punk rock as possible. Howard himself says, "The book *Against Nature* by Huysmans had been part of my college course reading, probably during the early days of Buzzcocks. The book talks a lot about the Symbolist and Decadent paintings, including Redon. Once I started looking at Redon's work I really liked his lithographs."

Linder elaborates, "There was a lot of bad collage around then for a few years. Or, maybe not bad, just obvious and workmanlike. Collage became to

the fanzine what candlewick was to the bedsit. By the time that Malcolm and I worked on *Shot By Both Sides,* I longed for a serif typeface. We used an old metal type font from the typesetting room at the Poly, and some of the decorative borders from there too." She continues, "But Magazine had nothing to do with collage and everything to do with a quality of light. How do you best show light? Through throwing a shadow. In my sketchbooks from 1977, I have careful copies that I made of the drawings of Odilon Redon, and this quote: 'Black is the healthiest of all colours'. I asked Howard to write something on the next page, and he wrote, 'You fill in some of the gaps for me.' The room that we tried to live our lives from was painted black – Howard had already done this before we lived together. All daylight was excluded by bedspreads at the windows; God knows now what the neighbours must have thought!"

The starting point for the *Touch And Go* sleeve was a series of Polaroid photos of the band taken by Linder – possibly after a gig at Eric's in Liverpool. Malcolm says, "I was always somebody that liked to relate the front cover to the back so I took the shape of my layout of the Polaroids on the back, and reflected them with the shapes I used on the front. Quite why it ended up pink and black I don't know. I think it was related to something inspired by Vogue magazine, although I can't think why. Perhaps the typeface I chose for the word Magazine – Modern No. 20 – felt quite like a fashion publication. When you're a younger designer you're less analytical. You do things more on instinct."

The sleeve for *Real Life* was born of late night conversations between Howard and Linder. She says, "We used to ponder the paintings of Gustave Moreau and wonder if we could create a timeline from Moreau's studio on the Rue de la Rochefoucauld, to our one room in Lower Broughton Road. Moreau painted Salomé in Paris in 1876, and I stuck an iron on a woman's head in Salford, a hundred years later." The *Real Life* cover was a monoprint of floating heads – once more referencing Odilon Redon. Linder explains, "Odilon Redon was one of our household gods. His quest to 'place the visible at the service of the invisible' seemed noble and timely, all the more so as the visual language of punk fell into cliché all around us."

Linder ripped a hundred or so pieces of paper into headlike shapes and then rolled four different inks onto the same glass plate that she'd used for making photomontages in 1976. Using a pencil and a light touch, she took each paper head, from pigment to pigment, drawing mouths and eyes onto the reverse of each, the pressure of the pencil collecting ink on the reverse side. She says, "By doing this, a series of tiny monoprints was created – a relatively archaic method of print making then. That method of producing an image was relatively random – Howard and I liked the artist being only partly responsible." Linder then made a series of larger black monoprints, and she and Howard selected one to serve as the chthonic background for the four faces saying, "It became

Real Life, somehow very local and very cosmic, all at the same time – Salford as Salomé, gazing upon the Apparition."

For the cover of third single, *Give Me Everything,* Howard chose another Redon image *(The Cactus Man)* and the design company that Virgin used at the time packaged it. *Rhythm Of Cruelty* was the first single released off the band's next album, *Secondhand Daylight.* With the design for the album cover yet to be finalised there are few obvious links between the artwork for the two records. Malcolm says, "I used a short filmstrip of images sideways across the sleeve. I can't really remember where they came from, or why I chose those particular images, although they suggest a kind of violent passion. It was the sense of rhythm from image to image that was clearly on my mind."

The front cover of *Secondhand Daylight* features an Ian Pollock image of a head on a stick that Howard happened across whilst browsing a Royal College of Art publication entitled *The Geek.* It caught his eye and the original coloured image informed the eventual colour scheme for the album. He says now, "I can't remember why its miserable brutality would have appealed. All I can say is: the search for images was never easy. When something caught my eye I tried to really take notice because I soon learned it wasn't always going to be easy to find an appropriate image."

Ian Pollock explains, "The image is a collage from elements of photographs I'd taken whilst researching the location of Brian Aldiss' illustrated novella *The Brothers of the Head* located along the Norfolk coast. I illustrated the book, which was published by Pierrot Publishing. The collage then went through various photocopyings to homogenise the grainy quality. The head on the post was from a photograph I took of a masked protestor at a 'Save the Whale' demonstration in Trafalgar Square. The resulting black and white image was then photocopied on a colour photocopying machine – a magic machine at the time, still in its infancy – which gave it a rich, subterranean quality."

Consulting his diaries from the time, Ian recalls, "Howard, excellent character of great intellectual vigour, rang me when I was living back 'up north' working on an illustrated version of the *I-Ching*. He said he was interested in my work and we arranged to meet. I took a folder of work to his less-than-opulent flat in Chorlton. He was aware of the Geek publication, focused in on the cover at the expense of the rest of my work, seemed to know what he was after, and expressed an interest in the graphic work of Odilon Redon. On 7 January 1979 he asked if he could use the *Geek* image on Magazine's forthcoming album and accompanying promotion. I have a record in my old accounts of a payment of £100 from Virgin Records dated 6 April 1979."

The gatefold sleeve came about partly because the band wanted to use the wide photo that Malcolm had commissioned. He introduced the band to photographer Richard Rayner-Canham, a recent graduate from St Martin's, who had constructed a unique camera in a wooden cigar box. A simple motor drive moved the film across a vertical slit, rather than a circular aperture, in order to take the shot. The exposure time was simply the length of time the motor ran, and the resulting transparency could be several inches long

The photosession was, by necessity, quite animated as the camera recorded any motion in front of it. The band were photographed by the round pond in Kensington Gardens walking, running and leaping across in front of the camera singly, one after the other. Because the film was capturing a sequence of connected moments in time, the images it produced could be quite distorted and somewhat bizarre. In the background were ducks and geese, similarly distorted into strange shapes. Many sequences were captured until it was decided they'd probably got the shot they wanted. As this was an experimental process, no one really knew how the photos would turn out. In the event one of the most restrained shots was eventually used for the sleeve, although others were used elsewhere as posters.

"The typeface I chose was called Melior." says Malcolm "I was looking for something more 'classical' than I'd used before, but still with a distinct individuality. On earlier sleeves we'd had a hard-hitting sans serif, some quirky Victoriana, and had alluded to 50s fashion. Both myself, and Peter Saville, with his early work for Factory, were now turning instinctively to sources other than modernist or contemporary styles for inspiration. I liked Melior because it was quite rounded and human, without any of the severity often associated with a more traditional font. I think this is probably the only time I ever used it."

Leading up to the release of *The Correct Use Of Soap,* the band made the decision to release several singles in quick succession. These all followed the same aesthetic and went on to influence the eventual design of the album sleeve.

Dave says, "In the 1950s records had cardboard sleeves – a carry over from 78s where records needed protection. A lot of record shops would keep the copies in the racks in those and then take them out and put them in paper sleeves. Because singles in 1979 didn't seem to be as important as they had been in the 50s and 60s I just thought if we recreated the cardboard sleeve it would just make them stand out a bit more."

Malcolm explains the problems this presented him: "First of all we couldn't match the 78s because they had glossy lacquered labels and it was impossible to do glossy labels with the contemporary manufacturing process. LPs had matt paper. We did go with the idea of having a cut out cardboard sleeve but there was an economic problem. Unlike Peter at Factory, who always just spent the money required for something out of the ordinary, because I was with a more mainstream label, with conventional production processes, I had to be slightly circumspect about how we went about doing things."

He continues, "For reasons of economy it was necessary for me to use the standard white card in stock at the pressing plant. In order to achieve a different but economically viable result I suggested, however, that we print on the other side, the 'wrong' side, which was a rough and ready brown, rather than pristine white. I was keen to use silkscreen printing and talked the record company into a two-colour silkscreen printed scheme on the wrong side of the card instead of having a conventional four colour scheme on the right side. The economics matched up: no extra for the card, and a compromise on the number of colours we would print. The bonus for me, along with the distinctive texture of the card, was that screenprinting ink was very dense, and was good for metallic ink, plus it was the only successful process for printing white on to the dark of the cardboard."

The aesthetic was thus born out of these different elements coming together. Each single in the series (*A Song From Under The Floorboards, Thank You (Falettinme Be Mice Elf Agin), Upside Down*) featured the same cardboard sleeve with silver printed on the dark side. The consistency of the colour of the card varied because of the nature of the manufacturing process itself and to distinguish them, each record label was a different colour. The album itself, *The Correct Use Of Soap,* used red and white with a distinctive chevron design. Sometime later, a blue and grey 4-track 12-inch EP was released, with all four title tracks (*Shot By Both Sides, Goldfinger, Give Me Everything* and *A Song From Under The Floorboards)* listed on the sleeve front in the typography from their original sleeves, but again printed on the wrong side of the card.

The live album *Play* features a photograph of the band at their Lots Road rehearsal space. The image, shot in a deliberately grainy style was taken by photographer and friend of the band Christina Birrer. The first set of photos Christina took featured John McGeoch but when the band decided to use one on the cover of *Play* they asked her to repeat the session with Robin Simon, who actually featured on the record. Howard says, "I liked the fact that the album was called *'Play'* and it was a live album with us playing on it (of course). But in the cover photo, although surrounded by instruments, we're actually not playing."

Malcolm's sleeve was deliberately austere, with a stark, modernist layout, which like the photograph, is in contrast to the dynamics of the music contained therein, as well a move on from the warmth and almost romantic feel that the sequence of sleeves for previous records had possessed. Malcolm says, "I was conscious of a deliberate attempt to almost mimic one of Peter's sleeves for Factory, but to 'play' with the cleanliness of the typography he might have used, both in the way the title on the front was uncomfortably offset, and the background colour on the reverse of the sleeve allowed for no margins at one edge. The choice of typeface was also challenging in its own way, neither 'classic' nor purely modernist."

The sleeve for *About The Weather* was in Howard's words: "My concept. Malcolm's execution." Malcolm elaborates, "The concept was clear: to represent a variety of types of weather – wind, rain, sunshine – all occurring at once in flurry of activity. The style was strictly diagrammatic, alluding to typical weather map imagery, and utilising recognisable symbols for the weather types illustrated. On reflection I do wish I'd commissioned an actual illustrator to produce these drawings, as to this day I am embarrassed about the crudity of my draughtsmanship. This was the first 12-inch single with a proper 'picture sleeve' that Magazine had released, and I liked the idea that the larger version of the sleeve had the same imagery as the 7-inch but with the simple addition of more border around the illustrations. So, although it was using the same components, the increased amount of space around the drawings gave it quite a different feel. I always approached a 12-inch sleeve as a new, but related, design challenge rather than a simple enlargement of the 7-inch."

The graphic style of *About The Weather* was very different from that of the album it was taken from. The photograph, which featured on the cover of *Magic Murder And The Weather* was chosen by Howard. He says, "It's like *The Geek*. One of those images I came across that stuck. This time in a photo book I flipped through circa 1977. In the book the photo was probably just titled *Mardi Gras* and I had no idea what Mardi Gras was. I probably thought it was a place name. I had no idea what was going in the picture except that it looked 'real' i.e. it was not a staged picture. That was a big part of the appeal. When it came to *Magic Murder And The Weather* cover time, that Bruce Gilden image was the only image I could think of that was remotely appropriate. In an ideal world I'd have liked something 'new' – not something, as it were, recycled from our past (namely a homemade leaflet for the Magazine Rafters gig, 1977). But, there again, given *Magic, Murder And The Weather* was to be our last album, there was a circularity about using it that I liked."

Malcolm says, "I devised a grid of vertical bars and wrapped the image all the way around the sleeve, perhaps subcosciously emphasising the circularity of having used the image before. I was always slightly averse to using something just as it was – that's a bit like using paint straight from the tin. I like to make things my own – the photo was a component that I worked with." Discussing the pastel colours used on the sleeve he explains that his use of colour was one way of keeping the visual identity of Buzzcocks and Magazine – who he describes as more "literary and sophisticated" – separate. He continues, "I always strived to produce something that wasn't just a pastiche of something else. For example, I didn't want *The Correct Use Of Soap* and the related singles to look exactly like copies of old 78s. I wanted to use that as a starting point and see where you could go to make it contemporary. Looking back, in purely commercial terms it isn't necessarily the best thing. People like to know their reference points."

He continues, "I figured if you really liked 'a' and you really liked 'b' and you mixed them together you'd get a new letter that isn't even in the alphabet. I'm often compared to my friend Peter. Peter was quite often the opposite. When he had a reference for 'a' he wanted to produce the most exquisite and deliciously executed version of that 'a'. He was always so precise and so spot on it caused a lot of people in the early days of his career to dismiss his work as merely pastiche. But it went way beyond that. It was all about the selection of what he wanted to use and his complete understanding of what it was about that that made him so special. It's his distillation of an idea that was so pure. That has since been understood and appreciated, but there was a long period of time where his work was dismissed for that. Instinctively I never really went down that route. I was always happy to try crazy collisions of ideas. Occasionally I did come up with something where you could say, 'That doesn't have a precedent.'"

By 1978, Malcolm had moved to London and set up his own graphic design studios Assorted Images, where most of the work for Magazine was produced. Some of the designs for the early Magazine compilations were done by one of Malcolm's senior designers, Damian Wayling, whilst later compilations used early Linder Sterling monoprints. Malcolm says, "I lost touch with the band in the late 80s, and I was a bit upset that when the four albums were issued for the first time on CD I wasn't permitted to do the repackaging. When you design a CD version of an album you can't just scale it down, as the graphic components need to work together on quite a different level. It's my view that as the designer of the original I would have been in the best position to make the amended versions. It saddened me. I was always very, very proud of the work I did for Magazine. I really did think it was some of my best and to have the control over reworking them in an appropriate way taken away from me was quite hurtful."

Malcolm's work for Magazine, Buzzcocks and other bands has been described as revolutionary on many fronts for its strong, abstract colourful style, the graphical branding of an artist and the use of all aspects of information on the sleeve – including catalogue numbers – as key components in his design. In the mid 1980s his studio was one of the first to substitute the computer workstation for the draftsman's table. In 1994 he founded multimedia agency AMX with Alasdair Scott, pioneering interactive design and media. Around 2003 he moved to Toronto as a designer of interfaces for interactive cinema, but returned to London in 2005 where he is now creative director at Applied Information Group.

Meanwhile Linder Sterling passed up the offer to design for Factory (recommending the younger Peter Saville instead) and also declined an invitation from Tony Wilson to record an EP for the label, with Ludus. Always confrontational and unafraid to express her sexual politics she continued to challenge the cultural expectations of women in her musical stage performances and cover art. Her fascination with female myth and sexual taboo manifested itself in the sleeve for *The Seduction* – which featured a woman wearing fishnet stockings, suspender belt and sanitary belt – and in a range of 'menstrual' jewellery – effectively beads and earings made to resemble bloodied tampons. From the mid 1980s she has concentrated on her provocative and thought-provoking visual and performance art with occasional and selective musical appearances.

When Magazine made the decision to reform in 2008, they turned once more to Malcolm Garrett to present the public face of the band. When designing the series of adverts that accompanied the February 2009 dates it was decided to draw on the typographic style of *The Correct Use Of Soap* era as it was felt that this would resonate with the largest number of fans. Whilst Malcolm was searching for the original font Vendôme, the word Magazine popped out of the screen set in Venus by accident, immediately grabbing his attention. It was decided to use this instead as "it looked really fresh, whilst maintaining the classic Magazine style."

From there the graphic requirements steadily expanded with two CDs, a range of posters and other merchandise needing to be produced to coincide with the February dates. Malcolm says, "I was very happy that we had quite quickly established a new visual language for this period in Magazine's career. It felt to me like a new chapter was beginning and to simply repurpose old designs didn't feel the right way to go." As Magazine picked up the pace with their summer festival appearances and gigs and looked forward to 2010, Malcolm continued to enjoy the opportunity to create visuals for a fresh collection of Magazine artefacts.

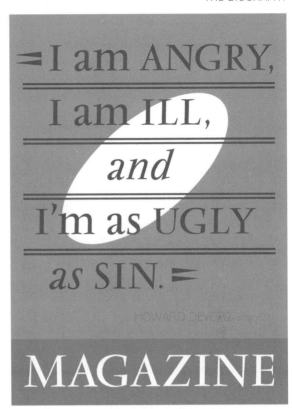

"I am ANGRY, I am ILL, and I'm as UGLY as SIN."

HOWARD DEVOTO

MAGAZINE

" I KNOW THE MEANING OF LIFE. IT DOESN'T HELP ME A BIT. "

HOWARD DEVOTO

MAGAZINE

Appendix One — **Lyrics**

... it even hurts when I scream

Definitive Gaze

I've got this bird's eye view
and it's in my brain
clarity has reared
its ugly head again
so this is real life
you're telling me
and everything
is where it ought to be

I like your nerve
I like watching you
but I don't watch what I'm doing
got better things to do
so this is real life
you're telling me
now I'm lost in shock
your face fits perfectly

My Tulpa

I suspect you ain't so sweet
as the lust I'm concealing
my skin wants to crawl back home to Ma
I've lost my way in my feelings

You always collect your fists
when my shadow falls upon your hands
you're just giving body heat away
but they say you're a nice enough young man

I want to see you
don't you want to see me?
I'm full of questions
you're full of mystery

You can touch yourself anytime
you can touch yourself anytime
I'm so wretched – you are so fetching
stop smiling at me – treat me unpleasantly

You've got the whole world in your wardrobe
your furniture's made to injure me
my skin will crawl back home to Ma
when our souls mingle uneasily

I want to see you
don't you want to see me?
I'm full of questions
you're full of mystery

Shot By Both Sides

This and that, they must be the same
what is legal is just what's real
what I'm given to understand
is exactly what I steal
I wormed my way into the heart of the crowd
I wormed my way into the heart of the crowd
I was shocked to find what was allowed
I didn't lose myself in the crowd

Shot by both sides
on the run to the outside of everything
shot by both sides
they must have come to a secret understanding

New offences always in my nerves
they're taking my time by force
they all sound the same when they scream
as a matter of course
I wormed my way into the heart of the crowd
I wormed my way into the heart of the crowd
I was shocked to find what was allowed
I didn't lose myself in the crowd

Shot by both sides
on the run to the outside of everything
shot by both sides
they must have come to a secret understanding

"Why are you so edgy, kid?"
asks the man with the voice
one thing follows another
you live and learn, you have no choice
I wormed my way into the heart of the crowd
I wormed my way into the heart of the crowd
I was shocked to find what was allowed
I didn't lose myself in the crowd

I didn't lose myself in the crowd
but I worm my way

Shot by both sides
I don't ask who's doing the shooting
shot by both sides
we must have come to a secret understanding

Recoil

Dashing through Paradise
so polite in what I say
lost in the age I'm in
I want a world to give away

I know what's mine
you'll learn what's yours
I know what you want to see
you scratch my back
and I grow claws
falling in love awkwardly

Dancing in my own good time
my words stick out of your face
if you're not feeling so weak today
somebody will take your place

I know what's mine
you'll learn what's yours
I know what you want to see
you scratch my back
and I grow claws
falling in love awkwardly

Burst

Once you had this promise
on the tip of your tongue
but it went without saying
it went on too long
all the straws you clutched at
have burst into flames
and so you smile that way
tantalisingly lame

The smart ones understand
how your heart bursts
like a bottle of champagne
your just desserts
the smart ones understand
you shouldn't settle for less
you're going to forget yourself
in my happiness

Keep your silence to yourself
(in my happiness)
you will forget yourself
(in my happiness)

Motorcade

I believe all that I read now
night has come off the corners
shadows flicker sweet and tame
dancing like crazy mourners
the man with the hotdogs sells lemonade
someone over there needs first aid
while me and the rest of the world
await the touch of the motorcade
no one finds time to turn a blind eye
you can't be too careful nowadays
and my friend says, "Listen…
to the stupid things they're making you say"

Here comes the motorcade
moving so slow and hard
like a snake in the closet
holding sway in the boulevard
here is your man
all faces turn unanimously
the small fry who sizzle in his veins
in all security

In the back of his car
into the null and void he shoots
the man at the centre of the motorcade
has learned to tie his boots
in the back of his car
in the null and void he sees
the man at the centre of the motorcade
can choose between coffee and tea

In the boulevard – the motorcade holds sway

The Great Beautician In The Sky

Laughter staggers on
in between their gags
pounding their faces
he's on his last legs

I don't care to dance
I don't care to dance
I don't want to dance
I'm not going to dance

Angels twitch nervously
the brave and the bold weep
we all want to know who
we should pay tribute to

Hey good looker
you could tell me all about it
go on – tell me all about it
I know your secrets
you could tell me all about it
go on – tell me all about it

I may have lost the thread
I was supposed to pull
may I say everyone
is irresistible

Everyone is irresistible
now I'm not sure which way I should turn
I can say "Now I've seen everything"
at last there must be no more to learn

That's what you want to hear
sadly, also it's true
and I know all your ways
and I'm still hung up on you

Oh great beautician in the sky
your innocence just saddens me
I shall throw it all against the wall
take my pleasure in spite of it all

I know your secrets
you could tell me all about it
go on – tell me all about it
hey good looker
I could fall all night all over you
hey good looker
roses are red, violets are blue

The Light Pours Out Of Me

Time flies
time crawls
like an insect
up and down the walls

The light pours out of me
the light pours out of me

The conspiracy
of silence ought
to revolutionise
my thought

The light pours out of me
the light pours out of me

The cold light of day
pours out of me
leaving me black
and so healthy

The light pours out of me
the light pours out of me

It jerks out of me
like blood
in this still life
heart beats up love

The light pours out of me
the light pours out of me

Parade

They will show me what I want to see
we will watch without grief
we stay one step ahead of relief
you tell me we've been praying
for a bright and clever hell
I think we've been forced to our knees but I can't tell

Sometimes I forget that we're supposed to be in love
sometimes I forget my position

It's so hot in here
what are they trying to hatch?
we must not be frail, we must watch
now that I'm out of touch with anger
now I have nothing to live up to
and I don't know when to stop joking
when I stop I hope I am with you

Sometimes I forget that we're supposed to be in love
sometimes I forget my position

What on earth is the size of my life?

My Mind Ain't So Open

My mind
it ain't so open
that anything
could crawl right in
my mind
it ain't so open
that anything
could crawl right in
the last place
to lose yourself
is in the world
where we all cling

Oh my lover
we are opening
windows we see
all that we see
overlooking
our vivid room
is it such a
dumb thing to do?
my life
happens around me
your life
happens around me too

Touch And Go

In the corner of your eye
I'm loitering with intent
you can tell me to move on
'cos all my money's spent
you're such a big girl
small world, isn't it?
you ask me what I do
well sometimes I stand
and sometimes I sit

Then you tell me so
it's touch and go
for now
why must it be so?
we'll touch and go
oh wow

You live in a big story
a party to all kinds of things
innerventing excuses, discovering new sins
you take a thousand liberties with me
saying "that's the price
for this kind of instant intimacy"

You strolled the pavements of a million dark hearts
flaunting your quality
patching up rows between fizgigs and demireps
you take your pleasures seriously

You offer me your hand
are you trying to catch something?
do you want to open me up?
do you want to close me in?

Give Me Everything

You're gonna give me immunity
you're gonna receive punishment
I'm gonna lose myself in you
because you're not quite of this world

There will be rooms
where we shouldn't meet
times I want to screw you up
and leave you in the street
you know everybody
you don't know a thing
you watch me in you
but I know what you're really seeing

With the eyes of the world upon you
you leave nothing to my imagination
and I leave nothing to be desired
'cos you're gonna feel like I feel

Now you give me everything
now you give me everything
now you give me everything
now give me everything

And I'll open up like a sliding door
oh so oblique and easy
oh you're so bleak and easy
'cos you're gonna feel like I feel

Now you give me everything
now you give me everything
now you give me everything
now give me everything

I beg of you
I beg of you
I beg of you

Feed The Enemy

It's always raining over the border
there's been a plane crash out there
in the wheatfields
they're picking up the pieces
we could go and look
and stare

How many friends have we over there?
the border guards fight unconvincingly
whatever we do
it seems things are arranged
we always have to feed the enemy

You could dance for me
and punch me through
you could dance for me
and punch me through
dance for me

We watched them trash the last camera
glued to all of our TVs
the actors on the replay
trying again to touch you and me

But they always seem to know
exactly what they're talking about
now they've got you in a corner
you've got no room to move
you've got no room for doubt
that's exactly what they're talking about
now they've got you in a corner
no room to move
no room for doubt

Rhythm Of Cruelty

I brought your face down on my head
it was something I rehearsed in a dream
you're too good looking for your own damn good
and you don't know what it could mean

You've got me dying of thirst in the meantime
it even hurts when I scream
you've got me drowning and still in the meantime
you don't know what it could mean

Because in my drunken stupor
I've got to admire your ingenuity
and nod my head oh so wisely
to the rhythm of your cruelty

You're oh so anguished now
you're oh so anguished now
you've got me dying of thirst in the meantime
it even hurts when I scream
you've got me drowning and still in the meantime
you don't know what it could mean

Because you want to have your price
and something you could hold your faith up to
I don't know how to tell you this
but you've got it coming all the way to you

You don't know what it could mean
you don't know what it could mean
I don't know what it could mean
we don't know what it could mean

Cut-Out Shapes

I enter the room
confident enough
for now I tread
a straight and narrow way
so I sleep soundly
a little blue in the face
cut-out shapes
in secondhand daylight

Somewhere else
something else
on my mind

She's caressing me
with the hidden hands
of the only kind of violence
she thinks I'll understand
we've got them dancing
to all of our confessions
they don't know how
we rehearse our dreams

Somewhere else
something else
on my mind
I just get numb
when you're hard to find

We met at a psychiatric unit
she was in for having habits
no-one else would try
she didn't know what she was in control of
she had all the advantages of magic
no-one could deny

There was an old lady
who swallowed a fly
your inescapable mother
such a crazy lover

I just get numb
when you're hard to find
I just get numb
when you're hard to find

Find out
you'll find out

Talk To The Body

You put me in the pictures
in the pictures in which my head is swimming
you were made for life
you're lost to the world
very transparent, very selfish
beautiful powerful careless women
watch it

My body screams yes
my mind just keeps its peace
clam up, calm down

We embrace during the journey
such a short ride in a borrowed car
the time is ripe for getting things right
at a very reminiscent temperature
watch it

My body screams yes
my mind just keeps its peace
clam up, calm down
clam up, calm down

I Wanted Your Heart

I wanted your heart
for the last time
I want to be in your bed
I want your words
to colour all that's been said
"I will love you when the devil is blind"
I wanted your heart
you didn't want mine

This is as close as I get
as I ever get
falling for things
I never thought
I'd find myself
falling for
as close as I get

Old ladies on the pavement
in the dense and empty hours
all as hard as nails
and brittle as pressed flowers
I was cold at an equally cold place
a cigarette between the flame and my face
you were laughing
like the goon squad in my heart
you were laughing
like the goon squad in my heart

This is as close as I get
as I ever get
falling for things
I never thought
I'd find myself
falling for
as close as I get

I wanted your heart
I wanted your heart

What do you think about
what I think about?
truths that are lies
when you spell them out
don't worry
don't betray the slightest emotion
yes I know
it's a separate emotion

As close as I get

Back To Nature

Back to nature
I can't go on like this
I want to walk where the power is
back to nature
I don't know where to start
back to nature
I don't have that kind of heart

Back to nature
back to somewhere else
back to nature
and right back on top of yourself
back to nature
I've got to look down
see where I am
or just hit the ground

And I'm telling you
I know what you've been going through
in my heart of hearts
when I was here
and you were there
nothing was between us

We're up in the air
we're down on the ground
we're up in the air
we're down on the ground

Here are your friends again
inching in the bedroom door
ah they want to touch me
and you show me their hands
how warm and soft and foreign they are
Cubans in surgical gloves
one on top of two on top of three
well I've got more than you

Back to nature
the voyeur will realise
this is not a sight for his sore eyes
back to nature
getting back at you
I couldn't act naturally if I wanted to

Back to nature
a trip that I can't take
people are thinking
that they've dreamed of this place
back to nature
it was somewhere else
back to nature
right back on top of yourself

And I'm telling you
I know what you've been going through
in my heart of hearts
when I was here
and you were there
nothing was between us

We're up in the air
we're down on the ground
we're up in the air
we're down on the ground

Believe That I Understand

Here is the love of your life
once again, once again
here is the love of your life
once again, once again
she fits the part
she fills the space
she'll never ever be out of place
she's got it all with her saintly face
another sick monkey
with a saintly face
another sick monkey
with a saintly face

Here is the lie of the land
once again, once again
here is the lie of the land
once again, once again
you squeeze yourself
out of your thin inner world
you squeeze yourself
out of your thin inner world
you squeeze yourself
into the big wide world
it's all in the hands
of your very best friends
it's good to agree
with the good guys again

You win some
then you lose some
you win some
then you lose some
put it out of your mind
put it out of your mind
you should look at me

So tell me your troubles again
and again and again
tell yourself not to do it again
and again and again
you want to touch me
show me your hands
you want to touch me
show me your hands
you want to touch me
show me your hands
you'd better believe that I understand
you'd better believe that I understand

Permafrost

Thunder shook loose hail
on the outhouse again
today I bumped into you again
I have no idea what you want
but there was something I meant to say

As the day stops dead
at the place where we're lost
I will drug you and fuck you
on the permafrost

There's not much that I miss
I'm far too forgetful for that
sugar's sweet some of the time
it's hard to keep some things in mind

As the day stops dead
at the place where we're lost
I will drug you and fuck you
on the permafrost

180

TV Baby

TV baby
I don't know what to think
TV baby
I don't know what to think
my mind's on the blink
I don't know what to think
TV baby
I don't know what to think

TV baby TV baby TV baby TV baby
I'm taking the leap for you
taking the leap for you
I leap for you
leap for you leap for you

TV baby–oh
be looking out for you

Because You're Frightened

You love me because you're frightened
and I'm falling in love with you
because I'm getting frightened
of the things you somehow make me do
you love me because you're frightened
I can easily believe my eyes
your fear is my finest hour
my fear is your disguise

Look what fear's done to my body
look what fear's done to my body

A frightening world
is an interesting world to be in
in the Forbidden City
or on The Roof of the World
or at the receiving end
of the nine o'clock news
however you put your mind to it
you can find fear where you choose

Look what fear's done to my body
look what fear's done to my body

You want to hurt
you want to crave
you want to praise and curse and blame
you want to believe just what you like
then you want to hurt and crave again

They took you to the top of the mountain
they showed you the valley
you bought it
you couldn't wait, could you?

Look what fear's done to my body
look what fear's done to my body

You want to hurt
you want to crave
you want to praise and curse and blame
you want to believe just what you like
then you want to hurt and crave again

You want to hurt and crave again
crave again

Model Worker

I'm sick of working on the land
I wanna work with machines and look handsome

I have been indulging
in ostentatious display
doing little more than eat
three square meals a day

And I've been shirking my duty
so I've been sending gifts to curry favour

But because I love you
and because you love me
a model worker
I'll willingly be

I need a holiday, I've not been well
take me to the Brocade River Hotel

And I just want to know
while the revolution lasts
will it enable me
to swallow broken glass?

I'm not too worried by hegemony
I know the cadre will look after me

And I just want to know while the revolution lasts
will it enable me to swallow broken glass?

I have been indulging in ostentatious display
doing little more than eat three square meals a day

But because I love you and because you love me
a model worker I'll willingly be

A model worker
I'll willingly be

I'm A Party

I'm such and such
I'm a scream
bad choices take me to task
you'll see
I'll take out the car
but nobody'll want to crash

Take me with you
I'm a party
I don't know where I've been
so all things being equal
I'm a party
I won't know where we're going

You could do me a favour
do whatever you want to
I will let you hurt me
because I know it hurts you
it hurts you

What you say goes
I'm a party
all over the town
I fell into you
I keep up with all that's coming down

So what's shaking?
I'm a party
you've got me racing, you've got me racing
the sound of a siren
in all the spaces between

You could do me a favour
do whatever you want to
I will let you hurt me
because I know it hurts you
it hurts you

I know it hurts you
I'm a party

You Never Knew Me

I don't want to turn around
and find I'd got it wrong
or that I should have been laughing all along
you're what keeps me alive
you're what's destroying me
do you want the truth or do you want your sanity?

You were hell
and everything else was just a mess
I found I'd stepped into the deepest unhappiness
we get back
I bleed into you
thank God that I don't love you
all of that's behind me now
still seems to be above you

I don't know
I don't know whether I ever knew you
but I know you
I know you never knew me
I don't know
I don't know whether I ever knew you
but I know you
I know you never knew me

Do you want to?

Hope doesn't serve me now
I don't move fast at all these days
you think you've understood
you're ignorant that way
I'm sorry, I'm sorry, I'm sorry
I'm sorry I can't be cancelled out like this
we had to kill too much
before we could even kiss

I don't know
I don't know whether I ever knew you
but I know you
I know you never knew me
I don't know
I don't know whether I ever knew you
but I know you
I know you never knew me

Do you want to?

Philadelphia

Your clean-living, clear-eyed
clever, level-headed brother says
he'll put all the screws
upon your newest lover
Buddha's in the fireplace
the truth's in drugs from Outer Space
maybe it's right to be nervous now

Who are these madmen?
what do they want from me?
with all of their straight-talk from their misery

Everything'd be just fine
if I had the right pastime
I'd've been Raskolnikov
but Mother Nature ripped me off
in Philadelphia
I'm sure that I felt healthier
maybe it's right to be nervous now

I had liberty of movement
but I'm so lazy
I'm so lazy
I'm just so lazy

You're just a big kid
you're not so big at that
you never got the hang of it
now you're being looked at

Where have I seen you before?
"Same place you saw me, I expect
I've got a good face for memories"
in Philadelphia
I'm sure that I felt healthier
maybe it's right to be nervous now

I Want To Burn Again

The newcomer arrives
possession and guilt in his face
apologises to the Customs man
for the gaping hole in his suitcase
says "I've seen where promises are made
I've seen how people are undone
it's always done
man to man
one to one"

I'm ditching an empty suitcase
I've been in Storytown
I've been swimming in poisons
been slowing up and down
I've known the eeriest wounds
the soul's long quarantine
when no rewards remain
no one and nothing comes clean

I've been blown about for years
on my way to you
I've been blown about for years
on my way to you
and I still turn to love
I want to burn again
and I still turn to love

In a room
where arrangements are made for success
you try to say that you possess me
by your caress
I met your lover yesterday
wearing some things I left at your place
singing a song that means a lot to me
I've known a certain grace

I've been blown about for years
on my way to you
I've been blown about for years
on my way to you
and I still turn to love
I want to burn again
and I still turn to love

I'm still turning
I want to burn again

Sweetheart Contract

We drank from cups on standard-issue sofas under scaffolding
informed sources said we were seen by observers – it's a meeting
I received an education
I was dominant for hours

I won myself a wealth of weapons, supermassive wealth
under a sweetheart contract which clearly stated
'Strength is always health'
I had one upper hand
I was dominant for hours

I want to be there, on the far side of sin
I've been putting myself through hell, waiting for hell to begin
I got insurance
I was dominant for hours

My tour-de-force is to forget all that's gone on around and about me
my manners are forever and whatever sells the newspapers suits me
I got an education
I was dominant for hours

I had one upper hand
I was dominant for hours

I got insurance
I was dominant for hours

We'd better give it back, it's not ours

Stuck

In the rush
the rush of my senses
in the heat
the heat of this moment
in the Palace of Nations
I think I can love you out of weakness

In the heat of this moment
I stick myself in laughter

Run for it
I'm running away
know-it-all
I will return again
pushing myself so helpless
hopeless
when I can love you out of weakness

Which of us is to blame?
I'm stupid
I only know enough to get out of the rain

Oh, I really tiptoe, I really tiptoe

Stop
when you cease to amaze me
take a look
my part in the pattern
I know it'll never matter
so I stick myself in laughter

I may love you out of weakness
is that what I was afraid of ?

A Song From Under The Floorboards

I am angry I am ill and I'm as ugly as sin
my irritability keeps me alive and kicking
I know the meaning of life, it doesn't help me a bit
I know beauty and I know a good thing when I see it

This is a song from under the floorboards
this is a song from where the wall is cracked
my force of habit, I am an insect
I have to confess I'm proud as hell of that fact

I know the highest and the best
I accord them all due respect
but the brightest jewel inside of me
glows with pleasure at my own stupidity

This is a song from under the floorboards
this is a song from where the wall is cracked
my force of habit, I am an insect
I have to confess I'm proud as hell of that fact

I used to make phantoms I could later chase
images of all that could be desired
then I got tired of counting all of these blessings
and then I just got tired

This is a song from under the floorboards
this is a song from where the wall is cracked
my force of habit, I am an insect
I have to confess I'm proud as hell of that fact

Habit

FOR F.D.

Twenty Years Ago

You turn pandemonium
into pantomime for one
twenty years ago I used your soap

So what!
you've got a name for it
yesterday goes on and on
inbetween the devil and the deep blue sea

You thrash about in your room
no space for thought
look no strings, look no strings
no visible means of support

Twenty years ago I used your soap

How did you ever come to move a muscle in this space?

The dollar's adrift

Twenty years ago I used your soap

The Book

This man is at the door of Hell... somehow it seems to be his destination after a life of subtle stubbornness. He doesn't expect to find himself waking up out of a dream... he doesn't expect to pinch himself and wake up and that kind of thing... in fact, the thought of that happening makes him smile. He's just mildly surprised to find himself there at the door of Hell.

To all accounts, the kindly old man who is the doorman (and who conceivably reminds him of his father) is sat reading a book... but he gets up smartly and without time for either of them to feel that they're standing on ceremony says, "Hold my book for a minute, would you, while I get the door open?" (Presumably, you know, you need two hands to open the door.) For some reason the old man doesn't just put his book down on the chair.

It all happens quite quickly... he finds that he's made a decision and is already holding the old man's book... as just about anybody else would have. But it seems a bit curious because... in however small a way you like to consider it... it is as if he's helping himself enter Hell... the path of least resistance. Of course, at the same time he suddenly thinks... even as he finally grips the book... "This is my chance for a reprieve ... the final test ... the straw which will tip the good deeds over the bad."

Next thing he knows, they have exchanged opinions on the book and he has handed it back to the old man and is being shown into Hell.

Upside Down

I think of the distance
between you and me
which doesn't explain
why the strangest places
still call my name
I don't know how to live
I only know how to disappear
and I don't want to travel
and I don't want to stay here

They speak of destiny and fate
and powers that move unseen
and I get these pictures
of how my life might have been
I hear home is where the heart is
but I never get to learn
where my heart is

Upside down
upside down
I'm always turning things
upside down

The timing was right
but it was still a surprise
to find my heart had followed my eyes
I was just another man
with his eyes on you
and a need for agony
that he had to subdue

Upside down
upside down
I'm always turning things
upside down

In your eyes

About The Weather

The weather's variable – so are you
changes, changes
but I can't do a thing about the weather
do you have your ticket?
can you foresee
changes, changes
another time when we might be together?

You have a broken window
through which the rain pours in my ear
this week's been all ears and edges
it's getting like a career

A chain of events
a change of heart
a chain of events
a change of heart

I will study your change of heart in depth

The weather's variable – so are you
changes, changes
but I can't do a thing about the weather
do you have your ticket?
can you foresee
changes, changes
another time when we might be together?

Now you're leaning on a fountain
with the sunshine on your shoes
you dislike the climate but you like the place
I hope you learn to live with what you choose

A chain of events
a change of heart
a chain of events
a change of heart

I will study your change of heart in depth

I'm so changeable – it's so frightening
I'm so changeable – it's so frightening

So Lucky

In this world of carelessness
there is delight, there is distress
a wilderness of mortal calm
sometimes ease, sometimes alarm

Lead me to a new world of comfort
lead me to a new world of comfort

Leave now quick, before you're missed
you can use the service lift
the neighbours're out on the morning shift
there needn't be the slightest risk

You know, we're lucky to be so important
you know, we're lucky it turned out that way
we are so lucky
we are so lucky

In this world of carelessness
there is delight, there is distress
we're never safe, that's for sure
the lucky shot through the open door

Lead me to a new world of comfort
lead me to a new world of comfort

so take your life in your hands and go
don't tell me where, I'd better not know
if I need to get in touch one day
I will employ the C.I.A.

Our love will equal the five year plan
like the harvest we'll cover the land
we are so lucky
we are so lucky

Lead me to a new world of comfort
lead me to a new world of comfort

The Honeymoon Killers

All police leave has been cancelled
we always imagine we're being followed

I saw an advert for ice cream
seems it was eaten in the Garden of Eden
I bought you one
you licked it slowly
and I got that certain feeling of freedom

Then we listened closely to some Mantovani
and waited for the cops to come

Vigilance

I'm in love with everything that's been left unsaid
that's gone down through the centuries
beginning
middle
and ending dead

I will forget
where I began
I'll lose track
I'll change hands
I'm not vigilant
it's no trouble
it's inevitable

It's so foggy at night always
and it's dark all day
all that has been hidden
will be shut off one day
until then I will attempt
whatever tempts me
tell me, is that good enough?
there's so much I can't see

I will forget
where I began
I'll lose track
I'll change hands
I'm not vigilant
it's no trouble
it's inevitable

You say in a little while
we'll have it all on file
my time ain't so vast
I can't spend it in the past

I will forget
where I began
I'll lose track
I'll change hands
I'm not vigilant
it's no trouble
it's inevitable

Come Alive

Bits of spirits were set on a carpet of carbon
pieces of apes were placed in a time of ice and iron

'Keep fit – Survive'
'Keep fit – Survive'

Primitive jeeps crushed fossils and ancient bone
chandelier-sized flowers aromatized pollen and chromosome
puzzles grew on trees where mutilated fruit hung
like the hats of inscrutable guests
who'd sipped their soft drinks and sung:

'Keep fit – Survive'
'Keep fit – Survive'
'You won't recognise yourself till you come alive'

Pepsi-Cola, Pepsi-Cola brings your ancestors back from the grave
Pepsi-Cola, Pepsi-Cola brings your ancestors back from the grave

At Leonardo da Vinci Intercontinental Airport
a Swiss pathologist missed his connecting flight

An asteroid kicked up the dust the dinosaur stubbornly bit
man's brain was taken
the cortex stuck at an awkward angle on it
his first words were:

"What have I done to deserve the sun?"
"What have I done to deserve the rain?"

Pepsi-Cola, Pepsi-Cola brings your ancestors back from the grave
Pepsi-Cola, Pepsi-Cola brings your ancestors back from the grave

The Great Man's Secrets

Forget about law
forget the crowded will
order will do
men are so easy to kill

A house of mistakes
a blood-filled flame
bad blood in motion
no proof to blame

The great man's secrets
the great man's secrets
the great man's secrets
the great man's secrets

Daily your dream becomes more of a nightmare to me
but I learned more than a hundred ways to fall asleep
our terror seems to be vanity
progress is hard with madness around your feet

The great man's secrets
the great man's secrets
the great man's secrets
the great man's secrets

In years to come all of this will be
nothing more than mystery to me

I was moved from one cell to another

I will leave by the same door I came in

The great man's secrets
the great man's secrets
the great man's secrets
the great man's secrets

In years to come all of this will be
nothing more than mystery to me

I must confess
I must admit
my executioner hasn't changed a bit

This Poison

My lifetime's habits will remain
this crush of hearts won't go away
tonight, one way, once and for all
good times aren't possible today

I took a little poison
I took it carefully
it built for me
a house on fire
this poison takes after me

This poison came too far to fail
desire unwinds in the last hour
within, the bed is overturned
my host, the antidote is sour

I took a little poison
I took it carefully
it built for me
a house on fire
this poison takes after me

Now put me down upon the lawn
right here – next to my favourite tree
I'm being foolish – can't you tell?
they all look just the same to me

I took a little poison
I took it carefully
it built for me
a house on fire
this poison takes after me

Naked Eye

She's wearing the shoes today
she's kicking her dog in the snow
she bought all three yesterday
she's the happiest person I know

When she's in a desert
when she's face to face with the sky
she can cast all the shadow she needs
with her naked eye

Suburban Rhonda

You urban vision of loveliness
moving scenes of skin
you understand the ways and means
of city discipline
a structured life in some girls' rooms
mirror glass and light
outside the landscape of power
dreams around appetites

Suburban Rhonda
don't be so smart
Suburban Rhonda
don't act so sharp
Suburban Rhonda
you'll wreck your heart
Suburban Rhonda
you'll wreck your heart

You could be just vain and live alone
on Separation Street
but if you did you know your life
would be incomplete
the tenements of disrepute
don't eye them longingly
I want to be the one
to put you out of your misery

Suburban Rhonda
don't be so smart
Suburban Rhonda
don't act so sharp
Suburban Rhonda
you'll wreck your heart
Suburban Rhonda
you'll wreck your heart

You'll wreck your heart

The Garden

I'm in a web
I TASTED BLOOD IN THE GARDEN
I'm in a maze, I'm in a maze
SO THEY HUNG SCIENCE IN MY HEART
I'm in a web
"YOUR PHONEY GHOSTS WENT BY" I LAUGHED
I'm in a maze, I'm in a maze
"I DRAGGED THEM OUT OF THE DARK"

I'm open wide
I PRESSED THORNS INTO MY FLESH
I am awake, I am awake
MY EYES LOOK LIKE CLAWS
I'm open wide
MAN EATING MAN EATING MAN
I am awake, I am awake
MY SICKNESS IS MY REWARD

I'm in a web
I'D SWEAR I SAW THE SUNLIGHT SHAKE
I'm in a maze, I'm in a maze
THE SKY'S ALL OVER MY HEAD
I'm in a web
I'M FEELING GRAVITY HARDEN
I'm in a maze, I'm in a maze
SOUNDING THE ALARM FROM THE CENTRE OF A FLOWERBED

I'm open wide
I AM THE ONLY ONE AWAKE
I am awake, I am awake
AND I'M SO WELL INFORMED
I'm open wide
I'LL SEE THE BOTTOM OF THE LAKE
I am awake, I am awake
IN THE EYE OF A BRAINSTORM

I AM RESPONSIBLE
I AM RESPONSIBLE
man eating man eating man
I AM RESPONSIBLE
I AM RESPONSIBLE

In The Dark

Keep it in the dark
you say now you want to stay

Put on your clothes
I think you should go away

I can lose my way on the shortest of journeys

Keep it in the dark
there is no defeating it

Put on your clothes
or I'm not eating it

I can lose my way on the shortest of journeys

The Operative

You were never found to be backward
or wanting in any way
you were hidden so cleverly in love
what scheme did you obey?

And I know why you go so slow
and I know why you go so slow
and I know why you go so slow

You had such strange disappointments
too bare against the paint
you knew the handle was broken
and your strong arm was faint

And I know why you go so slow
and I know why you go so slow
and I know why you go so slow

Your tired empire's fallen
victim to your unease
you could make yourself so useful
if you'd get on your knees

And I know why you go so slow
and I know why you go so slow
and I know why you go so slow

Appendix Two — **Chronology**

October 1977 – June 1981

1977

2 October : Electric Circus, Manchester *(3 numbers)*

28 October : Rafters, Manchester *(official debut)*

31 October : Recording contract with Virgin signed

14 November : Queen Elizabeth Ballroom, Belle Vue, Manchester (recorded for *So It Goes*)

December : Bob Dickinson leaves

1978

January : Dave Formula joins

16 January : *Shot By Both Sides/My Mind Ain't So Open* – 7-inch single

First UK Tour

24 January : 100 Club, London

25 January : Sandpipers, Nottingham

26 January : Rafters, Manchester

27 January : Eric's, Liverpool

30 January : Nashville, London

31 January : Barbarella's, Birmingham

1 February : F Club, Leeds

14 February : John Peel Session recorded for BBC Radio
Touch And Go, The Light Pours Out Of Me, Real Life, My Mind Ain't So Open

February : *Top of the Pops,* BBC TV
Shot By Both Sides

14 April : *Touch And Go/Goldfinger* – 7-inch single

Spring UK Tour

24 April : Satellite City, Glasgow

25 April : Eric's, Liverpool

26 April : Barbarella's, Birmingham

27 April : Tiffany's, Bristol

28 April : Metro, Plymouth

30 April : Greyhound, Croydon

5 May : Sheffield Polytechnic

6 May : Cardiff University

7 May : Roundhouse, London

8 May : Ritz, Manchester

6 June : Publishing contract with Virgin signed

9 June : *Real Life* – Album

Summer UK Tour – (Real Life Tour)
[support: The Zones]:
1 July : Barbarellas, Birmingham *(cancelled)*
2 July : Coatham Bowl, Redcar
3 July : Clouds, Edinburgh
5 July : St George's Hall, Bradford
6 July : Locarno, Coventry
7 July : Russell Club, Manchester
8 July : Eric's, Liverpool *(2 shows with teenagers-only matinee)*
9 July : Top Rank, Sheffield
10 July : Outlook, Doncaster
12 July : Town Hall, Torquay
13 July : Metro, Plymouth
14 July : Colston Hall, Bristol
15 July : Friars, Aylesbury
16 July : Odeon, Canterbury
21 July : Lesser Free Trade Hall, Manchester
[with Buzzcocks for 2nd year anniversary] (filmed by Granada)

24 July : John Peel Session recorded for BBC Radio
       Give Me Everything, Burst, I Love You, You Big Dummy, Boredom

28 July : JB's, Dudley
29 July : Barbarella's, Birmingham
30 July : Lyceum, London

August : Martin Jackson leaves, Paul Spencer joins

2 August : Eric's, Liverpool

European Tour
[supporting Patti Smith]
5 September : Philipshalle , Düsseldorf
6 September : Statthalle, Bremen
7 September : Hemmerlein-Halle, Nuremburg
8 September : Noewelt, Berlin
9 September : Noewelt, Berlin
11 September : Friedrich Ebert Halle, Ludwigshafen
12 September : Circus Krone, Munich
13 September : Circus Krone, Munich
14 September : Rheine Main Halle, Wiesbaden
15 September : Concert House, Vienna
18 September : Forest National, Brussels
21 September : Paradiso, Amsterdam
18 September : L'Empire Theatre, Paris (filmed for French TV) [with Magma]

September : *Old Grey Whistle Test* , BBC TV
       Definitive Gaze, Give Me Everything

October : Paul Spencer leaves, John Doyle joins

17 November : *Give Me Everything / I Love You, You Big Dummy* – 7-inch single

UK Tour
21 November : Locarno, Portsmouth
22 November : *In Concert* recorded for BBC Radio *(producer Jeff Griffin)*
23 November : The Venue, London *(2 shows)*
24 November : The Venue, London *(2 shows)*
[with Neo]:
25 November : Manchester University
27 November : Metro, Plymouth
28 November : Locarno, Bristol
29 November : Mountford Hall, Liverpool
30 November : Lancaster University
1 December : Newcastle University
2 December : King's Hall, Derby
3 December : Town Hall, Middlesborough *(cancelled)*
4 December : Sheffield University
5 December : Leeds Polytechnic
6 December : Barbarella's, Birmingham
7 December : Locarno, Coventry
8 December : Pavillion, West Runton
9 December : Friars, Aylesbury
10 December : Top Rank, Cardiff

12 December : Brussels TV 'Folllies' [with Gruppo Sportivo]

16 December : Russell Club, Manchester (recorded)

1979

Warm-up Tour – (Rhythm Of Cruelty Tour)
26 February : Sussex University, Brighton
27 February : Leicester University
28 February : Wolverhampton Polytechnic
1 March : Keele University
2 March : Brunel University, Uxbridge
3 March : Essex University, Colchester
5 March : Cambridge University
6 March : Lincoln College
7 March : York University
8 March : Strathclyde University, Glasgow
9 March : Hull University
10 March : Huddersfield College

2 March : *Rhythm of Cruelty / TV Baby* – 7-inch single
30 March : *Secondhand Daylight* – Album

Secondhand Daylight Tour UK
[special guests: Simple Minds]
16 April : Winter Gardens, Malvern
17 April : King George's Hall, Blackburn
18 April : Top Rank, Sheffield
19 April : De Montford Hall, Leicester
20 April : Clouds, Edinburgh
21 April : Aberdeen University
22 April : St Andrews University
23 April : Apollo, Manchester
25 April : City Hall, Newcastle
26 April : Victoria Hall, Hanley
27 April : Odeon, Birmingham
28 April : Gaumont, Southampton
29 April : New Theatre, Oxford
30 April : Colston Hall, Bristol
1 May : Exeter University
2 May : Theatre Royal, Drury Lane, London
3 May : Odeon, Canterbury
4 May : Corn Exchange, Cambridge
5 May : Leeds University [with Simple Minds and The Human League]
6 May : Empire, Liverpool

18 May : John Peel Session recorded for BBC Radio
　　　　　TV Baby, 'Thank you', Permafrost

European Tour
9 May : Ancienne Belgique, Brussels
10 May : Vorduit, Gent
11 May : Hotel de Ville, Charleroi
12 May : Salle de Rencontre, nr Nancy
13 May : Le Palace, Paris
14 May : Salle des Concerts, Le Mans
15 May : Salle des Fêtes, nr Cleremont Ferrand
16 May : TV show, Madrid
17 May : Barcelona
18 May : Theatre le Madeleine, Marseilles
19 May : Faculte de Lettres, Nice
20 May : Salle Pierre Lamy, Annecy
21 May : Ecole Speciale d'Architecture, Paris

American 'Alien' Tour
28 July : The Hot Club, Philadelphia
29 July : Bayou, Washington DC
1 August : Hurrah, NYC
2 August : Hurrah, NYC
3 August : West Hartford [with the Ramones]
4 August : Paradise Club, Boston
6 August : Oxford Ale House, Newhaven

7 August : Albany

8 August : Syracuse

9 August : Pretzel Enchaine, Montreal

10 August : The Edge, Toronto

11 August : The Edge, Toronto

12 August : After Dark, Buffalo, NY

14 August : Real World, Cleveland

15 August : Bookies, Detroit

17 August : Mothers, Chicago

18 August : Mothers, Chicago

19 August : Gary, Illinois

20 August : Zaks, Milwaukee

21 August : Long Horn, Minneapolis

23 August : St Louis

24 August : The Palladium, Dallas, Texas

25 August : Armadillo World Headquarters, Austin, Texas

26 August : Opera House, Houston, Texas

30 August : The Whiskey, Los Angeles

31 August : The Whiskey, Los Angeles

1 September : The Whiskey, Los Angeles

2 September : Cuckoo's Nest, Costa Mesa, California

3 September : Santa Barbara

4 September : Old Waldorf's, San Francisco

5 September : Old Waldorf's, San Francisco

8 September : Seattle

10 September : Commodore, Vancouver

Quickly arranged 'secret' warm-up gigs prior to recording '*Soap*'

13 December : Loughborough University [supporting The Mekons]

14 December : JB's, Dudley *(secret billing as 'Colour Supplement')*

1980

7 January : John Peel Session recorded for BBC Radio
A Song From Under The Floorboards, Twenty Years Ago,
Look What Fear's Done To My Body, Model Worker

8 February : *Song From Under The Floorboards/Twenty Years Ago* – 7-inch single

7 March : *Thank You (Falletinme Be Mice Elf Agin)/The Book* – 7-inch single

UK Tour

23 April : Royal Iris ferry, Liverpool

26 April : Mountford Hall, Liverpool

27 April : Pavilion, Ayr

28 April : Astoria, Edinburgh

29 April : Tiffany's, Glasgow

[with Bauhaus]:

30 April : Sheffield Polytechnic

1 May : Lyceum, London

2 May : Guildhall, Northampton
3 May : Russell Club, Manchester
4 May : Unity Hall, Wakefield
5 May : Wellington Club, Hull
6 May : Digbeth Civic Hall, Birmingham
7 May : Trinity Hall, Bristol
8 May : Ajanta Cinema, Derby
9 May : Leeds University
10 May : Surrey University

May : *Upside Down/The Light Pours Out Of Me* – 7-inch single
May : *The Correct Use Of Soap* – Album

European Tour
14 May : Barcelona [with Lene Lovich]
22 May : Bataclan, Paris
23 May : Salle des Fêtes du Baron, Orleans
24 May : Salle Europa, Metz
26 May : Palais D'hiver, Lyon
27 May : Patinoire, Grenoble
29 May : Amphi Descartes, Poitiers
6 June : Eindhoven, Holland
7 June : Velp, Holland
8 June : Festival of Fools, Amsterdam

18 July : *Sweetheart Contract*, *Feed The Enemy* (live), *Twenty Years Ago* (live),
          Shot By Both Sides (live) – Double 7-inch single
          Sweetheart Contract, *Feed The Enemy* (live), *Twenty Years Ago* (live),
          Shot By Both Sides (live) – 12-inch single
          Sweetheart Contract/Feed The Enemy (live) – 7-inch single

July : John McGeoch leaves, Robin Simon joins

North American Tour
5 August : Ontario Theatre, Washington DC
6 August : Hurrah, NYC
7 August : The Bottomline, NYC
8 August : Club 57 (Irving Plaza), NYC
9 August : Emerald City, Cherry Hill, New Jersey (nr Philadelphia)
10 August : The Main Act, Lynn (nr Boston)
12 August : Commodore Ballroom, Vancouver
13 August : Paramount Theatre, Seattle
15 August : Fox Warfield Theatre, San Francisco
16 August : Civic Avenue, Santa Monica
19 August : Tuts, Chicago
20 August : Bookies, Detroit
21 August : Danforth Music Hall, Toronto
23 August : Paramount, Denver

New Zealand / Australian Tour

28 August : Mainstreet, Auckland

30 August : Mainstreet, Auckland

3 September : Checquers, Sydney

5 September : Thebarton Town Hall, Adelaide

6 September : Festival Hall, Melbourne

7 September : Macy's Hotel, Melbourne

10 September : Central Club, Melbourne

11 September : Geelong University, Melbourne

12 September : Bombay Rock, Melbourne

13 September : Crystal Ballroom, Melbourne

16 September : National University, Canberra

17 September : Newcastle Ambassador Nightclub, Sydney

19 September : Festival Hall, Brisbane

20 September : Family Inn, Sydney

21 September : University of New South Wales, Sydney

22 September : Bexley North, Sydney

24 September : Rockgarden, Sydney

25 September : Macquarie University, Sydney

26 September : Royal Antler Hotel, Sydney

27 September : Sylvania, Sydney

30 October : Metropol, Berlin

December : Robin Simon leaves

December : *Play* – Album

1981

January : Ben Mandelson joins.

5 January : *About The Weather/In The Dark* – 7-inch single
About The Weather/In The Dark/The Operative – 12-inch single

30 May : Howard Devoto issues 'leaving' statement

June : *Magic, Murder And The Weather* – Album

Appendix Three — **Discography**

Studio Albums

Real Life

V2100 – UK, Virgin, 9 June 1978 – LP – 9 tracks :
Definitive Gaze, My Tulpa, Shot By Both Sides, Recoil, Burst, Motorcade, The Great Beautician In The Sky, The Light Pours Out Of Me, Parade

OVED62 – UK, Virgin – LP – 9 tracks: as V2100

V12100 – USA, Virgin, 1978 – LP – 9 tracks: as V2100

CDV2100 – UK, Virgin, 1988 – CD – 9 tracks: as V2100

CAR01808-2 – USA, Caroline, 1991 – CD – 9 tracks: as V2100

VJCP-68806 – Japan, Virgin, 2007 – CD – 13 tracks, 9 tracks: as V2100 plus:
Shot By Both Sides (single), *My Mind Ain't So Open, Touch And Go, Goldfinger*

CDVR2100 – UK, Virgin, 2007 – CD – 13 tracks: as VJCP-68806

Secondhand Daylight

V2121 – UK, Virgin, 30 March 1979 – LP – 9 tracks:
Feed The Enemy, Rhythm Of Cruelty, Cut Out Shapes, Talk To The Body, I Wanted Your Heart, The Thin Air, Back To Nature, Believe That I Understand, Permafrost

* VIP-6936 – Japan, Virgin, 1979 (promo) – LP – 9 tracks: as V2121

V12121 – USA, Virgin, 1979 – LP – 9 tracks: as V2121

* VIP-6936 – Japan, Virgin, 1979 – LP – 9 tracks: as V2121

CDV2121 – UK, Virgin, 1988 – CD – 9 tracks: as V2121

CAR01809-2 – USA, Caroline, 1991 – CD – 9 tracks: as V2121

VJCP-68807 – Japan, Virgin, 2007 – CD – 13 tracks, 9 tracks: as V2121 plus:
Give Me Everything, I Love You, You Big Dummy, Rhythm Of Cruelty (single), *TV Baby*

CDVR – UK, Virgin EMI, 2007 – CD – 13 tracks: as VJCP-68807